1001

❧ Tips ❧
for
Canadian
Gardeners

Patricia Hanbidge

Alison Beck, Laura Peters & Don Williamson

LONE PINE

Lone Pine Publishing

The Distributor: Lone Pine Publishing

Library and Archives Canada Cataloguing in Publication

Hanbidge, Patricia
1001 tips for Canadian gardeners / Patricia Hanbidge ; with Alison
Beck, Laura Peters and Don Williamson.

   Includes index.
   978-1-55105-593-0

   1. Gardening--Canada--Miscellanea. I. Beck, Alison, 1971- II. Peters, Laura, 1968- II. Williamson, Don, 1962- IV. Title. V. Title: One
thousand one tips for Canadian gardeners.

SB453.3.C2H353 2008   635.0971   C2008-901386-7

Editorial Director: Nancy Foulds
Project Editor: Sheila Quinlan
Production Manager: Gene Longson
Design & Layout: Michael Cooke, Heather Markham
Cover Design: Gerry Dotto

PC:*P1*

Contents

Acknowledgements

I would like to extend my thanks to my husband and my daughters for their patience and continued support in the many pursuits horticulture has taken me! Thanks also to the rest of my family for always being flexible and willing to pitch in any way they can. Thanks to editor Sheila Quinlan who had the daunting task of making sense out of what I wrote—my thanks for all your time and patience. To my fellow writers, I feel proud to write alongside all of you.

I would like to dedicate this book to the gardeners who unselfishly shared with me their secrets for the good of gardeners everywhere. I feel honoured to have the opportunity to make my contribution through this book to gardeners both near and far. May *1001 Tips for Canadian Gardeners* be one of your most useful gardening books!

—Pat Hanbidge

I'd like to thank the many people who've offered me gardening tips over the years and most particularly my family for their excellent tips in all aspects of my life.

—Alison Beck

Collecting gardening tips is great fun and simply not possible without the guidance and expertise of the gardeners I've been fortunate to learn from over the years. Never stop gardening or learning and always have fun!

—Laura Peters

I would like to express my appreciation to all the wonderful people involved in this project and to the many sources of information and inspiration that helped fill this book with all the great information that you see here. I also thank The Creator.

—Don Williamson

Planning

All successful gardeners are also good planners. Winston Churchill said it all when he said, "Those who plan do better than those who do not plan, even though they rarely stick to their plan." This quote epitomizes gardeners. How many times have you envisioned your garden in your mind—only to find that the final result is not quite the same as you dreamed it?

General Planning Tips

You might need a little bit of help sorting out your dream garden, so here are a few places to start.

- Go to a nearby park, garden centre, arboretum or botanical garden, where the plants are labelled and unusual specimens are grown—it will show you what thrives. What is growing there is the best guide to what will grow in your area.

- Walk through your neighbourhood and look around at what other gardeners are growing. You might see interesting and unusual plants that you hadn't noticed before, or plants that you were told wouldn't grow in your area.

- Note what plants you like and what is in bloom when. Strive to learn as much as you can about the plants you want to grow to see if they are appropriate for your environment and landscape.

January is a great time for garden planning. It is often too cold to do much outside, and as the seed catalogues flood your mailbox, you can dream of your

7

garden in spring without interruption. In winter, the bones of the garden are laid bare, so you can take a good look at the garden's overall structure without other features interfering.

It does not matter whether you are starting with a blank canvas or you've inherited someone else's garden—you still need to have a plan. **Imagine the garden you'd like to have, and keep a notebook and your diagrams at hand so you can jot down ideas as they come to you.** Just remember that the plan is only your guideline; a garden is all about living things, so it rarely turns out exactly as you envision it.

Keep a journal of your garden. Note everything you see, such as when plants emerge from winter dormancy, when they flower, how well the plants are performing and your maintenance practices. A plan is only as good as the amount of preparation and diligence that has been put into it, and a journal will help you to better plan for the next gardening year.

Pay extra attention if it is your first chance to observe your garden for an entire growing season. It takes at least a full year to settle into a new landscape. **Notice the microclimates and think about how you can put them to good use.** Are any areas always quick to dry? Do some areas stay wet longer than others? What area is the most sheltered? You can cater your plantings to the microclimates of your garden.

Create an overhead drawing of your property to use for planning the landscape design and any renovations. Use graph paper to plot out the location of the house and any outbuildings, features such as sidewalks, driveways and patios, the location of trees and shrubs (mark out where the trunks and drip lines are), the location of flower beds, the location of your vegetable garden, shaded and sunny areas, wet and dry areas, different soil types and the location of utilities (both

8

above and below ground). The closer you can get to a scale of the exact measurements that exist on the property, the better. You can have separate maps for each garden area if you have a large property. Make copies and use them to keep track of your plans. Create a master plan and then sub-plans so you can keep track of the changes you'd like to make, and do make, each year.

Implement a landscape plan one phase at a time to ensure that enough time and money are invested to do that phase well. It is much less overwhelming to work on one part of the plan than to try to do the whole thing all at once. Remember that each completed phase will require yearly (or more frequent) maintenance. Avoid installing more landscape than you can properly maintain.

It is amazing how the years go by so quickly. **If you make a drawing of specific use areas, you will be surprised at just how often you reference the plan.** For example, if you make a plan of just your vegetable garden, you can plan and keep track of crop rotations. A plan of your perennial beds will allow you to look up that plant you just can't seem to remember the name of.

Site Analysis

Once you have a map of your yard, gather information about your site. It may seem like a lot of work, but it only needs doing once, and the benefits are great. **Doing a detailed site analysis will help guide you to make appropriate choices, such as which plant species to choose and whether you will be able to install the plants and hardscape features yourself, or if hiring a professional would be more appropriate.** Include as much of the following information as possible:

- the type of soil on your property and whether the soil type is the same for all areas (include all the results of your soil tests)

- the drainage patterns and location of drainage tile, if installed

- the location of your water source, whether it is a tap or an underground system, including the location of the irrigation sprinkler heads and their state of operation

- any elevation change such as a slope or depression

- the sunny and shaded areas of your landscape, with seasonal variations included

- traffic patterns, including lawn traffic

- landscape areas such as planting beds, lawns, patios, sidewalks and water features

- all current and historical information about maintenance practices

- any information about past pest problems, when those problems happened and what action was taken

- any other problem area that is not pest related.

Keep track of problem areas in the garden. Note any exposed and sheltered areas. Determine where prevailing winds are coming from, and note windswept areas that could benefit from a shrub, fence or hedge for shelter. Indicate areas where snow is quick to melt, thus losing benefit from the protection of the snow, and snowbound areas, where the snow is slowest to melt.

Planning Considerations

In order to really be successful in planning your garden, you need to begin with a goal. It's like planning a trip. You usually decide what your destination will be first, and then plan how you will get there. **So, before you buy anything to put into your garden, consider what it is you want to achieve.** Once you have your dream garden firmly ensconced in your mind, then it is time to do the fun part—the actual gardening itself.

Plan for the Long Term

Consider your entire family, now and into the future, when planning your garden. Will you have a lawn, and how big does the lawn need to be for the desired usage? Is space necessary for your kids to play or for your dog to run? Do you entertain in your outdoor living space? Are you allotting an area to sit, to relax, to eat? Can space in the landscape be left for a future swimming pool, rock garden, pond or fire pit? Now is the time to try to look into the future and determine what your needs might be months and years later. Although it is difficult, part of planning for the present is planning for the future.

A well-designed, attractive landscape will increase your property value. **Some landscaping features, such as an underground irrigation system, covered patio or landscape lighting, will add more value to your home than the cost of installation.** So not only are you creating a wonderful outdoor living space, but you are also making an investment in your property. What a nice way to do financial planning. You just need to remember two words: curb appeal.

Trees, shrubs and features such as fences, arbours, patios, sidewalks and fire pits make up the permanent structure of the garden. **Select these elements carefully; they are some of the most visual parts of the**

landscape throughout the year, so they need to be attractive in winter as well as summer and relatively easy to maintain.

Pathways through your garden allow all parts to be viewed and explored, and they allow for ease of maintenance. Stepping stones, bark mulch, gravel and paving bricks make excellent paths. Consider that gravel and mulch paths may need to be topped up occasionally, which increases the maintenance that is needed in the garden. **When choosing the material for the "flooring" of your landscape, it is a good idea to do some shopping around.** Items that will be an integral part of the landscape for a long time need to be of good enough quality to last the duration. Rather than buying a less expensive flooring material that might last only 10 years, it is sometimes prudent to buy a bit more expensive material that will last for a longer period of time. Don't forget to count the labour it takes to install the material as part of the total cost.

Consider how your outdoor living area influences the indoor living space. A well-placed deciduous tree saves energy and money by keeping the house cool and shaded in summer but allowing much-appreciated warmth and light from the sun through in winter. Evergreen species can be used as a barrier to keep the wind from blasting onto your house in winter, thereby keeping your house warmer as well. Woody plants also prevent soil erosion, retain soil moisture, reduce noise and filter the air.

Remember that your needs of your garden will change over time. Children grow up and no longer need the same kind of play area. Changes in your work away from home may give you more or less time in the garden. The best garden plans will not only suit your needs now, but will easily morph to suit your future needs.

Plan to Accommodate Growing Conditions

Consider the growing conditions in your garden before you select, buy or plant anything. The amount of sun, shade and rainfall are key to ensuring that whatever you decide to plant will survive. The type and fertility of the soil will be the determining factor to plants thriving rather than just surviving. The length of the growing season and the topography will of course also influence the types of plants you select, and the locations in which you plant them.

Think of your landscapes and gardens as works in progress, regardless of their current state. As gardens mature, the growing conditions change. For example, what was once a sunny bed may now be shaded by the tree that was planted years ago, and the plants that thrived in the sunny bed are no longer appropriate.

The single most important thing you can do when planning is to make sure you have the right plant in the right location. Consider the mature size of the plant and its cultural requirements. Resist the urge to plant any selection in a location that will not allow it to thrive. Instead, adjust the plan to accommodate planting each plant where it will grow best.

For any specific conditions, whether they are hot, dry areas or low-lying, damp sections, select plants that prefer those conditions. The plants will be healthier and less susceptible to problems if they are grown in optimum conditions. Some plants considered high maintenance become low maintenance when grown in the right conditions.

Knowing your growing conditions can prevent costly landscaping and planting mistakes—plan ahead rather than correct later. Making a mistake on a paper plan is easy to correct by simply erasing that tree you planted. However, in the garden, to move a tree is a little bit more

13

difficult. If you are unsure of your growing conditions, experiment with annuals to help you learn about the conditions in your garden. Once you feel more confident, you can plant perennials, trees and shrubs.

Plan to Maintain Your Garden

Determine how much time you want to spend in your garden now and into the future. In order to be happy with the end result of your planning, you need to ensure that you do not become a slave to your garden. **Envision how much maintenance your finished garden will require. That amount should mirror the amount you're prepared to spend.** Think about every bit of maintenance required, including cutting the grass, pruning the trees, hoeing the weeds, watering... and even the removal of plants that don't make it. If you enjoy your time in the garden keeping everything in check, then you might want to include plants that take a little bit more care. If your time is limited, then maybe low-maintenance plants are the best choice.

While you are planning, think about how much turf you have in your landscape. Turf or lawn areas require a lot of maintenance. To have a healthy, weed-free lawn, you need to ensure that it gets adequate moisture and fertilizer throughout the growing season. However, many municipalities routinely limit the amount of water you can use in the landscape. **Consider alternatives to grass in areas that are not really used.** There are many alternatives to turf with the same appeal that traditional grass gives to a landscape. Alternative groundcovers and xeriscapes are being hailed as the way of the future.

Plan for Year-Round Interest

One of the most desired elements of a garden is to have colour for as long as possible. It is possible to create a garden that has some plants in bloom all season long; all it takes is a bit of planning.

However, bloom time is not the only thing to consider. In more northern climes especially, year-round interest is an important component when planning your garden. We often get caught up in planning only for the growing season, which leaves many months when the garden is not really thought of. Many Canadians have a growing season as short as 100 frost-free days; for the other 265 days, there is not much growing in the landscape. Gardeners with short growing seasons need to become adept at designing for those other seasons. Think about how you could make your landscape more interesting during the long, cold winter. **Consider the flowering times of your plants, but also whether they provide any fall colour or if they have any architectural appeal in the winter months when the rest of the garden is buried in snow.**

Fall is one of the most beautiful seasons, with wonderfully warm days, cool nights and less of those pesky bugs that have been hanging around all summer. Some years, Mother Nature gives a beautiful fall so we can enjoy the most brilliant colours in the landscape. **Think of every single plant in your landscape and whether or not it has any fall appeal.** It might be difficult at first to remember to think about the colour of the leaves in your landscape, but leaf colour is an important element to consider when landscaping.

When planning your garden, try to get added landscape value with every plant you choose. Consider the attractiveness during the growing season, but think about other features that might be possible as well. Try to plan prior to planting to mix the fall colours attractively together. Place brilliant reds with happy yellows. Remember that in areas that don't always have those nice red colours, there will always be lots of yellow, orange and every shade of brown.

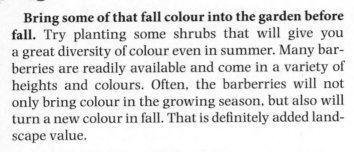

Bring some of that fall colour into the garden before fall. Try planting some shrubs that will give you a great diversity of colour even in summer. Many barberries are readily available and come in a variety of heights and colours. Often, the barberries will not only bring colour in the growing season, but also will turn a new colour in fall. That is definitely added landscape value.

In the middle of winter and into early spring, there may not be very much colour in the landscape, but the snow is beautiful. It covers the drab landscape in a white blanket that shimmers like diamonds when the sun shines. Snow lets us forget for awhile all of our outside chores—out of sight, out of mind. So if only for that reason alone, we welcome our snowy blanket. However, if you live in an urban area, that beautiful white very quickly becomes shades of grey. **Choose plants that will bring new life and colour to your landscape in all seasons.** Consider persistent fruit, unusual bark and branch patterns, evergreens and colourfully stemmed shrubs as winter interest in your garden design.

In areas where winter is long, it is extra important to plan for it. Take a few moments to really look at your landscape. **Look at it from the outside when you park your car, and look at it from the inside through the windows you most often look out of; then decide on the areas that need sprucing up.**

Select colours and textures that you find pleasing. You will get more landscape value if you group your trees and shrubs together, using each individual attribute to enhance the other. For example, planting red- or yellow-twig dogwoods in front of dark green evergreens will make both the green and the coloured bark stand out.

Here are a few selections you might consider to help get rid of the grey:

- river birch (*Betula nigra*) has very ornamental bark

- Siberian coral dogwood (*Cornus alba* 'Siberica') has upright, red stems with soft, green foliage

- American bittersweet (*Celastrus scandens*) is a woody vine that has persistent clusters of orange fruit

- sea buckthorn (*Hippophae rhamnoides*) has fine, silvery green leaves with clusters of orange fruit that persist all winter

- Annabelle hydrangea (*Hydrangea arborescens* 'Annabelle') has large, showy, white blooms in midsummer that dry on the stems to provide winter interest

- barberry (*Berberis* spp.) has foliage ranging from beautiful yellow to crimson.

Features such as birdbaths, ponds, benches, decks and winding pathways improve the look and function of your garden year-round. Even if the element is not really functional, it can still be attractive.

Environmental Factors

Sunlight

Pay close attention to sunlight and where it falls through the day and year. It will help you determine what should be planted where, based on light, and is also important when creating summer shade in your outdoor living areas. In order to shade your patio area with a tree, that tree needs to be planted in the proper location. Remember that the sun will be in a different location in summer and winter. Planning can be a little bit more difficult when it is being done in the winter months, as our observations report the winter sunshine areas instead of the more important summer sunshine areas, so update your observations of sunlight during the growing season.

Be aware of the amount of sunlight that reaches all parts of your garden. Available light is affected by buildings, trees, fences and the position of the sun at different times of the day and year. Trees are not the only plants that can shade a planting bed. Tall, sun-loving plants such as sunflowers may provide shade for other plants. Temporary shade can be achieved by covering a trellis with tall, fast-growing morning glories, scarlet runner beans or hops. Knowing what light is available in your garden will help you determine where to place plants adapted to different light levels.

Carefully plan to allow for the best and most appropriate light to reach your chosen plants. Work with nature. It is always better to match the plants to your garden rather than modifying your garden's existing conditions to match the plants. If your plants tend to be thin and leggy with sparse foliage and few flowers, they are probably getting less sunlight than they require and are therefore more prone to attacks by insects and disease. Plants that get more sun than they require may suffer from dehydration and scorched foliage and are also more prone to attacks by insects and disease.

There are four categories of light in a garden. Full sun locations, such as south-facing walls, receive direct sunlight at least six hours per day. Partial shade (partial sun) locations, such as east- or west-facing walls, receive direct sunlight for four to six hours of the day and shade for the rest. Light shade locations receive shade most or all of the day, but some sunlight does filter through to ground level. The ground under a small-leaved tree, such as a birch, is often considered to be in light shade. Full shade locations, such as north-facing walls, receive no direct sunlight.

The intensity of full sun and the depth of full shade can vary. For example, heat can become trapped and magnified between buildings, baking all but the most heat-tolerant plants in a concrete oven. Conversely, that shaded, sheltered hollow that protects your heat-hating plants in the humid summer heat may become a frost trap in winter, killing tender plants that should otherwise survive.

Climate

Climate is the term given to all of the meteorological conditions in a particular area, including temperature, precipitation and wind. Knowledge of your climate is invaluable when planning a landscape. Hardiness zone maps are available. These maps show in detail the lowest temperatures that can be expected in a year. Average annual minimum temperatures are based on the lowest temperatures recorded for a number of years in each area. **Use this information as a guide to what plants will easily survive in an area, and ensure that a component of your landscape is made up of plants that are sure to survive.**

Use local information sources for fine-tuning your decisions. Your favourite local garden centre is a great resource, and information such as the last frost date you can expect is important. However, there will

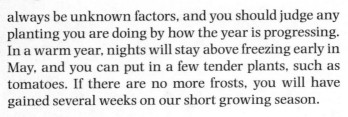

always be unknown factors, and you should judge any planting you are doing by how the year is progressing. In a warm year, nights will stay above freezing early in May, and you can put in a few tender plants, such as tomatoes. If there are no more frosts, you will have gained several weeks on our short growing season.

Microclimates

Create and use microclimates—small areas that may be more or less favourable for growing different plants—in the shelter of a nearby building or stand of evergreen trees, in a low, still hollow, on top of a barren, windswept hill or close to a large body of water. For example, a south-facing, sheltered wall or grotto creates an area that warms up sooner in spring and stays warmer for more hours in a day than the rest of the garden, making it an ideal place for plants that need more heat than the rest of the garden can provide. These specialty areas will allow you to grow more tender plants than would survive elsewhere in your hardiness zone.

Consider planting a windbreak, especially on the side of your property that the prevailing winds blow in from. Strong winds can cause physical damage by breaking weak branches, shredding herbaceous foliage and stems or blowing entire trees over. It is best to choose windbreak trees from among the species that can flex in the wind, and to plant them far enough from buildings to avoid extensive property damage if they or their branches fall.

Be aware of the problem areas in your garden and use the knowledge of the microclimates to turn those problem areas into opportunities. **If you have a damp area, instead of moaning about it, turn it into your own little bog garden.** Dig out the damp area 35–50 cm (14–20") below ground level, line it with a piece of punctured pond liner and fill it with soil. The soil will stay wet but will still allow some water to drain away, providing a perfect location to plant moisture-loving perennials.

If you have a very exposed area in your garden, you can make a planting that will shelter the area, or you can find plants that will do well there. A hedge or group of trees or shrubs will break the wind and provide an attractive feature for your garden, but if a living windbreak is not a possibility, use plants that will work for the exposed situation. For instance, if you are trying to plant a perennial border in an area on the southwest side of your property that gets wind and sun, there are many plants that will easily thrive under those conditions. Drought-resistant plants have different morphological conditions that allow them to lose less water than other plants, and therefore can survive under drier conditions.

If an area of your garden always seems dry, consider a xeriscape planting. A xeriscaped area can be just as attractive as a conventional garden—it simply depends on how you plan it. Many plants are drought resistant and thrive even in areas that are never watered. Yarrow, hollyhock, prickly pear cactus, black-eyed Susan, jack pine, potentilla, lilac and cosmos are just a few of the possibilities for a dry section of the garden.

Topography

Slope has a great influence on the planting site. **Think about if there are areas in your landscape appropriate for the features and plants you want to install.** For example, relatively flat areas with good drainage in full sun are great for lawns and planting beds and are the easiest to maintain. Sloped areas, depending on the amount of the slope, will need appropriate plants that can handle rapid drainage and/or help bind the soil together to prevent erosion.

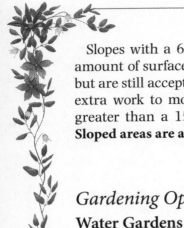

Slopes with a 6–15% grade will have an increased amount of surface runoff during irrigation or rainfall but are still acceptable for grass. These slopes will take extra work to mow, water and fertilize. Slopes with greater than a 15% grade are best for other plants. **Sloped areas are also good candidates for terracing.**

Gardening Options and Trends

Water Gardens

Water gardens are a possibility for anyone, even a gardener without a yard to garden in. The easiest and most economical water garden is one that can be created in a container for the deck or balcony. Many ready-made container water gardens are available, or you can create your own. Garden centres have lots of water garden supplies, and many water plants will grow as well in a large tub as they will in a pond. **Use your imagination to create a unique water feature anywhere you desire.**

An easy but spectacular water feature for your deck starts out as two pots: one that is quite large and one that is smaller. Fill the large pot with water, and place the small pot on a stand inside the large pot. Fill the small pot with water, add a few water plants and a small pump to circulate the water, and *voila*—you have created a water feature that will be envied by all your garden guests.

If a container water garden is not quite enough for you, then there are many other choices. **Consider what it is you would like to create with the water feature in your landscape, and plan accordingly.**

The first step to including a water garden in your landscape is to determine the best possible location. Having a water garden close to the areas you frequent is almost always the best choice so that it may be enjoyed the maximum amount of time. Water gardens are most often created on relatively level ground in a sheltered spot that gets full sunlight.

Size and shape are the next big decisions to make. The water feature should complement the overall landscape, so the existing garden design will in part determine the size and shape of the pond. The size will then determine the number and types of plants and fish the pond will accommodate.

There are several types of liner to choose from for your water feature. **Choose between concrete, a preformed liner and a flexible liner.** Concrete is the oldest material used to construct water features, and the most expensive, but when installed correctly, it is very durable. A preformed pond may be the easiest alternative if you are looking for an in-ground pond that will be relatively inexpensive and easy to install. There are many shapes and sizes available to fit a variety of landscapes. A flexible liner is another alternative to concrete; it will likely cost less, can be made to fit any shape and can be mended if it leaks. All three types have pros and cons, and more options within the option, so do your research; then decide which is best for you.

Next, you will need to decide on a pump and filtration system. Pumps are used to circulate water through the pond. They oxygenate the water, operate a fountain or move water to the top of a waterfall or stream and are often used in conjunction with a filtration system. A filtration system is used to remove unwanted matter, such as floating or decomposing debris, algae or excess nutrients, from the pond. When choosing filters, be sure to take into account their ease of servicing as well as their maximum flow rate.

Water gardening should be fun. Having a pond opens up a huge variety of possible plants for all gardeners.

Be adventurous and create a unique and beautiful water feature that reflects your own personality and the things that you like best in the garden.

Container Gardens

Anyone with a little bit of space can enjoy gardening in containers. **Regardless of what you like to grow, you can do it almost as easily in a container as in the ground.** It only takes a little bit of planning to ensure a good crop—even on a balcony.

If you garden in containers, you get the benefit of the beauty, scent and even harvest of plants with less labour than a conventional ground-based garden would take. A container is generally smaller than a garden in the ground, so the maintenance of your container garden is less labour intensive because your soil to till is rather limited.

Container gardening can easily be geared to varied levels of mobility. For many elderly people, making the small adjustment from traditional gardening to gardening in containers is a way to continue their love of gardening. People in wheelchairs or those who cannot bend down to the ground can garden in relative comfort using containers placed at an accessible height.

You may find yourself having to move your home at an inopportune time of year. There may not be time to prepare a traditional garden that would enable you to enjoy fresh greens or herbs. Again, the solution is container gardening. **Containers can be planted wherever you are and easily moved with you so that your gardening season is uninterrupted.**

Consider gardening in containers to extend the gardening season. You can get an early start in spring without the transplant shock that many plants suffer when moved outdoors, and you can protect tender plants from an early fall frost by moving the containers into a garage or shed. Also, when winter just seems too long and you need to grow something or go mad, a simple solution is to grow something indoors. Take advantage of a bright windowsill and grow herbs indoors year-round.

The only real disadvantage of container gardening is the need to water more frequently during hot and dry spells. If you are a gardener who runs away for part of the growing season, it will be necessary for someone to come in and water your container gardens. Using the largest container possible will minimize this small inconvenience, but it is necessary to remember that water is definitely essential.

Containers can be used throughout the landscape. **With careful positioning, a group of varied and different containers can have a great impact.** Move the containers slightly away from one another as the plants mature to allow space in between the containers for the plants to fill and so the sun can reach the leaves. Containers placed in a triangular outline often look best, either with a tall or large container in the middle with smaller pots on each side, or a tall container on one end with successively smaller containers sloping down to the other end.

If you want a formal container design, consider an even number of plants or features. Mark the front entrance of a house with a pair of square pots, or plant two rows of tall, narrow trees to form an allée.

If your garden is less formal and more polychromatic, then a scattering of odd containers is quite a nice addition. Collect a variety of interesting vessels that can double as containers for your favourite plants. Scatter them throughout the landscape by themselves or in groupings, creating focal points or simply a little bit of interest. If you like modern, eclectic and contemporary settings, use repeated plantings with an odd number of plants and focal points.

Don't forget about the landscape on a higher level. **Hanging plants add a wonderful effect to the landscape.** A row of hanging baskets will look most attractive when all the containers are identical; however, the plantings do not need to be the exactly the same.

Choose containers that will fit the theme or the feel of the garden as a whole. The container itself is really only the vessel that holds the medium you plant into. Any container will work as long as it has some kind of drainage capability.

Theme Gardens

A popular trend is to plant a theme garden. **Let your artistic side go wild, and imagine all kinds of possibilities.** Your favourite sports team colours could come alive in your garden and become the talk of the neighbourhood. Only the availability of suitable plants will limit your dreams. Any theme will work as long as you include only plants that will thrive under similar cultural conditions.

Theme gardens can be a lot of fun to design but don't always work out well. A good example of a theme garden that is doomed to fail is a cat garden. It seems like a great idea for a theme, what with the many plants that include something about cats in their name—cattail, pussy willow, pussy toe and catmint, to name a few—and there are many gardeners with a great love for cats. However, not even those four plants will all grow well under the same conditions. **To have a successful theme garden, it is essential that the plants chosen will all be able to grow well in the same area.** In this case, cattails like to be under water and pussy toes thrive in dry areas—end of theme.

A romantic garden could be fun. Many people consider roses to be romantic, so they could definitely work with this theme. Include plants such as Cupid's dart, love lies bleeding and bleeding heart. Fragrance is important for setting a romantic mood. Heliotrope has beautiful blue flowers paired with a vanilla-like scent. Sweet alyssum has a honey-like, sweet scent. White flowers bring romance to the night, as they will look almost luminous in the moonlight. Datura, lilies and nicotiana are also great choices for night viewing.

How about an animal garden? If you have young gardeners, this is a really fun theme garden. Include plants that are named after animals, and for once in your garden, don't worry about dandelions.

A sensory garden would be challenging but also very rewarding. Target all the senses, and choose plants that will thrill one or more of the senses. Textured plants such as lambs' ears and wooly thyme are unforgettable after you touch them. Experiment with a variety of scents such as spicy rose, lavender, mint, basil and the cornucopia of scented geraniums. Don't forget about sound; include plants that move with the air. Think about the sound of grasses blowing in the breeze or the sound of poplar leaves in a summer windstorm.

Try using native plants. There are so many reasons to "go native." Native ecosystems are much more complex than we can hope to copy in a garden. However, by learning more about native plants, you will learn to appreciate the diversity of the native habitat. By including native plants in your landscape, you are creating habitats for native wildlife species as well as maintaining the native plant species themselves. Native plants are already adapted to your area and tend to thrive with minimal maintenance. They have managed to survive for countless years without any more care than Mother Nature gives, so from the maintenance standpoint alone, native plants are worth growing.

Shade gardens require less maintenance than a garden in full sun. Plants do not grow as quickly, so the amount of watering and weeding is often reduced.

Years ago, it was difficult to find enough plants to create a really attractive shade area; that is not the case anymore. Shade gardens seem to have a tranquility that is unequalled in sunnier areas, and they can very easily become your favourite areas in the landscape.

Produce your own food in a vegetable garden. Plant vegetables that you will enjoy eating. It is satisfying to go through the process of sowing the seeds, tending the plants and harvesting the food to cook for your family and friends. Take that joy a little bit further and, when planning your vegetable garden, consider planting extra to donate to a local food bank or homeless shelter. Even if you just end up with the inevitable extra zucchinis and tomatoes, they can be put to good use.

Some other themes could be a herb garden, a rainbow garden or even a pizza garden or tea garden. The pizza garden could consist of garlic, tomatoes, green peppers and onions all grown in wedge shaped pieces to form a giant pizza. A tea garden could be fun, complete with tea pots or kettles as garden features. Combine lemon verbena, peppermint, fennel and lemongrass, add a table and chairs and have tea in the tea garden.

Healing Gardens

The therapeutic benefit of gardens is well known. Even images of natural spaces and gardens help reduce stress. Gardens have been healing places throughout time. The only gardens that survived medieval times were herbariums enclosed in monasteries or castles. The gardens most often contained medicinal and culinary herbs. The garden as a healing place diminished with the modernization of the world, but rising interest in alternative therapies has helped the resurgence of the healing garden. **Healing gardens are one of the most popular trends in gardening today.**

A healing garden can be really any kind of garden that helps you feel better, safer, less stressed and even more comfortable. Evoke these feelings with a garden that is attractive, low maintenance, functional and economically and environmentally sound.

A simplistic design is more conducive to healing than a chaotic one. Create enough variety to provide interest but not so much as to be unsettling. Any transitions should appear to be almost effortless; your eye should easily flow from one area to another.

Paths through a healing garden should be beautiful but functional. Provide enough space for walking and for wheelchairs, if needed. If people in wheelchairs are going to be using the garden, the paths should be about 1.5 m (5') wide. Use smooth, even surfaces that will not be slippery when wet. Paths should not be steep enough to make walking difficult. You should be able to stroll through the garden, not hike through it.

A healing garden will work only if it is peaceful. Create some spaces within the garden that are more private so you have places to rest or contemplate. Keep out intrusive noises with the help of thick, lush vegetation and a small water feature. The sound of running water is soothing and will drown out unwelcome sounds.

Outdoor Rooms

One of the latest trends in the gardening industry is to create outdoor rooms in the garden. Outdoor rooms are a transition space between indoor comforts and outdoor elements. Outdoor rooms require sturdy flooring, such as bricks, flagstones or wood decking, and some form of wall or border to define the space. Outdoor rooms usually have a specific function for which they are designed.

If you live in an urban setting, consider a covered patio or outdoor space; it protects you from the elements and from the prying eyes of your neighbours. This cover can be as simple as the large umbrella that often comes with patio furniture or as elaborate as a pergola covered with your favourite vine.

You often see a garage on the front of the house that extends out from the front door and creates a bit of an outdoor room. Capitalize on the structure by adding an arbour or pergola, which can then be used to support vines, hanging baskets and other container plants. If there is room, you could add a chair or two, or even a small bistro table.

Design your outdoor rooms to match or complement the décor and design of the interior of your home, which allows a smooth transition when moving from indoors to outdoors and vice-versa. These outdoor rooms may not have year-round use, but a well-designed area will tame the elements enough to allow for a longer season of use than the more open areas of the garden.

Garden Labyrinths

A recent (or ancient, depending on how you look at it) trend in gardening is to create a labyrinth. Labyrinths have been around for thousands of years in many different forms and are found in almost every major religious tradition around the world as places for reflection, prayer and comfort. In gardens, a labyrinth can be a place to meditate, or it can be a place to go for a pleasant walk.

A labyrinth is not a maze. A maze has many dead ends and is a challenge to find your way through. A labyrinth consists of only one path that leads into the centre and back out again, though there are certainly many twists and turns. There are, of course,

some basic designs available for you to reference if you are planning to build your own labyrinth. The path can be made with stone, bricks or a more natural material such as a hardy groundcover. Border the path with any type of hedge. Decide how high you want your labyrinth walls to be, and choose plants that will reach that height.

Design Tips

Unity is the goal for every landscape design. The best landscapes in the world appear to be wholly planned from start to finish. They are, of course, never totally planned, but all of the components blend together to create the whole unit. The man-made structures blend with the rhythm of natural landforms planted with vegetation that is diverse but harmonious. This unity results from the combination of all the principles of landscape design.

It is easy to plan for a visually appealing garden, but it takes a little bit more thought to remember all those other senses. Scents in the garden are a very personal preference. If you and your family like to enjoy scented areas, there is a multitude of plants available. It can be extremely nice to have scented selections in areas of the garden that you use at night, when scented plants are most aromatic. It is quite romantic to have a late-evening dinner in the garden surrounded by the heady scents we relate to more tropical climes. **Make sure your plan has features and plants that stimulate not only sight and smell, but also hearing and touch.** The latter two are a little more difficult to plan for than the other senses, but you can add supple plants that move and rustle in the wind, water features, birdbaths and wind chimes to hear and plants with soft, fuzzy textures to touch.

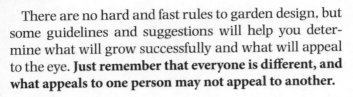

There are no hard and fast rules to garden design, but some guidelines and suggestions will help you determine what will grow successfully and what will appeal to the eye. **Just remember that everyone is different, and what appeals to one person may not appeal to another.**

Style

Decide fairly early in your garden plan on the style of garden you would like to have. Will it be a formal or informal design? Formal designs often have straight paths and bilateral symmetry and are best in large spaces. Informal designs use curved paths and lines and often appear to lack symmetry. The current trend is to enjoy less formal designs in our garden areas. This informal approach often requires a little bit less maintenance.

If you are just beginning to landscape, you may not know what you really like or dislike. **If you are having trouble finding your style, brew a big pot of tea and take some time to look through some garden magazines.** You will see parts of gardens that you find attractive. Look at those parts and determine what it is you like about them. Are they formal or informal? Do they have bright colours or are they more subdued? Are there added features that attract you? As you begin to notice what specific things you find attractive, you will find your style emerging.

Regardless of the style you choose, some variety is important. Combining different features creates interest and contrast in your garden. Depending on your personal tastes, you may like a lot of variety or you may like a calmer, more serene space. Either way, too much variety can be chaotic, but not enough variety can be monotonous. Strive to find the balance between the two extremes.

Colour

Colour is often the first thing we notice in a garden, so choose your colours carefully. When planning for colour in the garden, you can choose plants that all flower at the same time, or whose flowering times are staggered. If you have an annual garden party, your focus might be to choose plants that will all bloom around the day of your party. Many gardeners enjoy seeing something in bloom all season long. Annuals will grow, mature and then give a beautiful bloom throughout the growing season, but not all perennials have a long season of bloom. If you are just starting out growing perennials, choose at least some plants that have a long bloom time. Perennials such as heliopsis and campanula will provide a long season of bloom and require very little care.

It is relatively easy to make a dramatic statement with colour; however, colour is a very personal choice. Many gardeners find it aesthetically pleasing to have harmonious colours or contrasting colours in their gardens, as opposed to the riotous blend often found in nature. Although Mother Nature seems to create a blend of all colours that looks quite wonderful, mortal designers do not always create the same beautiful blends.

Different colours have different effects on our senses. Cool colours, such as blue, purple and green, are soothing and can make small spaces seem bigger. Warm colours, such as red, orange and yellow, are more stimulating and appear to fill large spaces. White combines well with any colour, and plants that bloom in white help keep the garden from becoming a blurry, tangled mess.

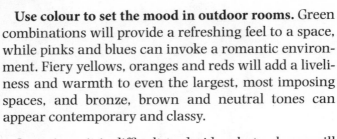

Use colour to set the mood in outdoor rooms. Green combinations will provide a refreshing feel to a space, while pinks and blues can invoke a romantic environment. Fiery yellows, oranges and reds will add a liveliness and warmth to even the largest, most imposing spaces, and bronze, brown and neutral tones can appear contemporary and classy.

Sometimes it is difficult to decide what colours will look good together. **Try using a colour wheel to help you choose what colour combinations you would like in your landscape.**

Colour echoing is using one colour, of various hues and intensities, throughout the garden to produce unity and flow. This has the effect of making it easy for your eyes to flow from one part of the garden to the next without abrupt changes. **Keep the colour of your house, outbuildings and structures such as fences in mind when deciding what colour or colours to use.**

Monochromatic designs use one colour that varies in hue and intensity, or colours very close to it on the colour wheel. For example, a monochromatic planting of yellow may include something yellow-green without disturbing the harmony of the planting. **Monochromatic designs can be difficult to do when starting out, so you might want to gradually work into doing monochromatic designs, starting with small areas in the landscape.**

Analogous colour designs use colours that are next to each other on the wheel—for example, using blues with violets and greens. Designing an analogous garden usually results in a soothing blend of colours. **Analogous colours add a little more spice to a design while maintaining the same mood of the planting.**

Complementary colour designs use colours that are opposite to each other on the colour wheel. These combinations make bold and dramatic plantings that are hard not to notice. **Colour combinations such as violet and yellow are relatively easy to design because there are lots of perennial plants with those colours.**

If you want an easy colour scheme, choose a poly-chromatic design. This type of design most closely resembles the mixture of colours and textures seemingly tossed together in a haphazard manner by Mother Nature.

Look for plants that come in dark shades very close to black. **The use of black, white and grey in planting designs helps make other colours really stand out, adds depth to smaller areas and plantings and helps tone down strong colours.** The colours that are included in the garden will become bigger and better by using these background colours.

Texture

Less noticeable, but important nonetheless, is texture in the garden. **To achieve different textures in a planting, look at the variety of foliage features.** Large leaves are considered coarsely textured. Their visibility from a greater distance makes spaces seem smaller and more shaded. Small leaves, or those that are minutely divided, are considered finely textured and create a sense of greater space and light. Using texture is one way of creating focal points. Our eye is drawn to fine textures, so designing a planting that uses finely textured plants can easily create a needed focus.

You can create myriad combinations with textures, colours and sizes of foliage. Flowers may come and go, but a garden planned with careful attention to foliage, using a mix of coarse, medium and fine textures, will always be interesting. Using foliage as a design tool will help create a visual appeal that is more subtle when the colours of the garden are muted.

Scale and Proportion

For the highest visual appeal, use the scale and proportion of your garden and its features to complement their surroundings. Your garden should be in scale with the permanent features in the landscape. A bungalow should have smaller trees surrounding it than a two-storey house. Large trees will dwarf a small house and make it appear smaller than it actually is. Within the planting area itself, features such as arbours should be of a size that complements the landscape as a whole.

Shape

Choose plants with different shapes to add variety to your garden and landscape. The careful use of shape can add drama and emotion or tranquility and peacefulness. Imagine the silhouette of a city skyline and how dull it would look if all the buildings were all square blocks of the same size. In a landscape, it is the plants that soften, enhance and essentially make that setting spectacular.

When designing a new bed within the landscape, create a shape that is complementary to the rest of the landscape. To decide on the shape of a new bed, place a garden hose on the ground in a shape you find attractive. Leave it in place for a few days so you have time to determine how it fits. If turf surrounds the bed, is it easy to mow around the current shape, or does the shape cause difficulties? The garden hose can be left in place while you dig, or replace it with temporary stakes or a line of spray paint where the hose was. You'll find spray paint especially useful when designing a bed with rounded edges.

Balance

If you have chosen to design a garden with more formal lines, you will likely have symmetrical balance in the garden. Symmetrical balance is the type of balance where a line can be drawn up the centre, and one side is the mirror image of the other. **Balanced plantings are pleasing to the eye but can be difficult to achieve.** Sometimes, one side of the landscape has very different growing conditions from the other, which makes it almost impossible to achieve a similar growth of plants on each side. In extreme cases, the mirror image is never attainable.

If you like the symmetry of a formal garden but do not want the entire garden to be formal, try including just a formal element in your garden. For instance, design your herb garden as a radial planting, with a central focal point and arms radiating out in all directions. Radial symmetry is achieved when all arms are balanced. This formal type of design dates back to the very earliest gardens that followed the Qur'an.

You can also design your garden to display asymmetrical balance: the two sides are not the same, but they have the same visual effect. An example of asymmetrical balance would be a tall, narrow plant flanked by a mid-sized oval plant on one side and a shorter, wider plant on the opposite side. This concept uses mass to balance the two sides of the landscape and is often easier to manage than symmetrical balance because differing growing conditions are easily managed by choosing plants that have different cultural needs.

Repetition

Tie the whole design together with colours or shapes that are repeated at intervals throughout the garden. Whether your design is on a large or small scale, identical, repeated plantings can be used to emphasize or exaggerate perspective along a pathway, entrance or succession of steps.

Sometimes you can get too much variety in the garden. This easily happens when you go to the garden centre without a shopping list and can't resist one of

everything that is for sale. This kind of design has so much variety that it is essential to bring a sense of continuity to that chaotic and unbalanced space. A simple solution is to create a row of identically planted containers. This provides appeal by filling an empty space that begs for a simple focus. Another trick is to place a succession of identical large containers that stand above in-ground plantings along a flower bed to create a stunning focal point.

For a more natural feel, design your garden with groups of the same plants planted in odd numbers. Random clusters of three to five flowering plants add colour and interest. You will get more bang for your buck with larger groupings of plants, which will give waves of colour or texture. Planting single selections will not give the same dramatic effect.

Use the repetition of shapes already in the landscape to help create a unified look overall. Look at the architecture, planting beds and walkways to determine what shapes already exist. Continue those patterns to blend existing and new elements in the landscape.

Vertical Elements
Plan for at least one strong, vertical focal point, which can draw your attention to a particularly beautiful part of the garden or away from an ugly view. Changes in elevation and contrasting colours and shapes are good methods for establishing a focal point. However, don't have too many focal points in your garden. One to three in a small garden are plenty. For areas of the garden that are viewed or used in many seasons, it is important to create that focal point in seasons other than summer.

🌳 Trees
Trees are the most important vertical element in any landscape, regardless of the season,

because they are visible year-round. **Carefully consider their location during your planning because trees usually prefer to be planted once and left alone.** It takes three years for plants to become established, so every time you move any plant, you will see a reduction of growth until it gets settled into its new location. Not only that, but also, while plants are getting established, they require more care, so moving a tree can increase the amount of maintenance your landscape will need.

Shrubs

One other vertical element in the landscape that is shorter in stature, shrubs are smaller than trees but still often very visible. **They are valuable parts of any design because they can easily tie together the tallest and shortest elements of the landscape.** They are important in the middle of the vertical landscape and can provide screening, control climatic conditions or even just bring a more vertical beauty to your yard.

For those designers wanting to get some colour into the garden in early spring, shrubs are the best way to do so. Think of spring-flowering shrubs such as the double flowering plum, whose spring blooms emerge before the leaves do. What a beautiful way to get colour in early spring. Evergreen shrubs will provide welcome colour during winter, when most everything else in the landscape is shades of grey.

Hedges

Hedges can be used in the landscape to delineate boundaries, provide privacy, block unpleasant views and provide shelter for other plants in the garden. If a hedge is placed in the correct location, it can also have great ornamental value,

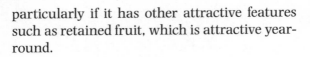

particularly if it has other attractive features such as retained fruit, which is attractive year-round.

Hedges and shelterbelts are great for minimizing noise pollution. You can also mask street noise with fences, water features or wind chimes. The plants do not really stop the sound waves, but a hedge will change the view, and when we don't see the cause of the noise, we don't notice the noise as much.

Vines

Vines can be woody, perennial or annual in nature. Woody and perennial vines have a longer life and will likely require a more elaborate support than annual vines. Vigorous annual vines can provide quick shade, instant screening, softening of hard edges, colourful flowers and even a good harvest of edible fruits. If you choose to add annual vines to your landscape, you have the ability to stay abreast with all the current trends. **You can change the feel of the whole area by simply growing a different vine.**

When growing vines, always consider what type of support structures will work the best. Woody vines get bigger and heavier each year and will need a large, very sturdy structure. Some folks consider chain-link fences to be ugly; however, they make excellent trellises. Be creative when erecting supports for your annual vines. Netting, string, bamboo poles, fancy lattices and any vertical structure can be used for annual vines. Netting and string can become almost invisible as the vines grow, allowing you to appreciate the beauty of the vine as a vertical element of the landscape without the structure adding to or taking away from it.

Some Common Design Problems

The landscape in front of your house is sometimes a difficult area to design. It is the part of the landscape that is first viewed, so it is everyone's first impression of you and your home. It is always exposed to the street and to the entire neighbourhood. You do not often spend much time in the front yard because it is really a public space; even working in your front yard, where everyone can see you, can be a bit uncomfortable sometimes. **So, do your best to make your front yard interesting and inviting, but low maintenance.** Neighbours and visitors should find it attractive. For you, the front landscape should be your first welcome back to your home. Consider the view from inside your house as well. It needs to be attractive...in, of course, all four seasons.

The front landscape should, in effect, frame your house. Trees and shrubs act in a similar fashion to the matting and frame on a picture. It is important that the areas surrounding the house help make the entire picture more pleasing to the eye. The plants in the landscape should also help accomplish the unified look.

You may find yourself with an overgrown landscape. An overgrown landscape is the result of poor planning many years ago, but it needs to be remedied. **Windows that were included in the design of the house to view the garden or to let in light should still be allowed that function.** Overgrown trees and shrubs blocking out light should be pruned. If the pruning leaves the shrub unsightly, then perhaps the plant should be removed completely.

The initial design of urban developments create another problem area. Alongside the house, there is usually a long, narrow area that resembles a bowling alley. Wind whips down these alleyways, and suitable

plant selections are limited by the space. However, these areas are the only way to unite the front and the backyard. **Try to give the illusion that your area is more than an outdoor hallway but actually a stroll through the landscape.** With the right plants, this space can be made to look shorter and less hallway-like, or, instead, like a long room. Break up that long space by creating interesting focal points along the way. If you have a sunny space, try a weeping caragana one-third or half-way down. Any type of weeping plant will not only draw the eye, but it will also direct the eye down and away from that long space.

House foundations are best covered or at least partially hidden. You do not need to plant right up to the foundation to achieve this. That area right against the house is devoid of moisture—a critical element for plant growth. Begin your planting outside the overhang to allow Mother Nature to provide at least some moisture. Try using a variety of groundcovers and other low-growing plants near the foundation to either enhance or screen the architecture. Likewise, on corners, use a branching type of plant to soften those very strong vertical lines.

Soil Preparation

Once you have a plan, it is time to put that plan into action. To do so takes preparation, and most preparation involves soil. But before you prepare your soil, you need to understand your soil.

Soil Basics

If you had to choose one element of the landscape that determines success, it would have to be the soil. You can be the best designer in the world, but if your design is implemented on soil that is substandard, the design will never achieve greatness. **It is important for you to gain a bit of basic knowledge of soil so you know how to improve or fix any potential problems.**

Soil and plants have a mutually beneficial relationship. Soil holds air, water, nutrients, organic matter and a variety of beneficial organisms. Plants depend upon these resources for their nutritional needs, and their roots use the soil as an anchor. In turn, plants influence soil development by breaking down large clods with their roots. Plants increase soil fertility by releasing by-products during their growth and by being recycled by soil microorganisms when they die.

There are hundreds of soil types and soil distribution patterns. Each soil type has a characteristic colour, texture, structure, mineral content, organic matter content, erosion potential, water permeability and depth. **Knowing the soil type will help you determine what kinds of plants will grow well there, whether amendments are needed and what type of maintenance regime is required.**

43

Soil Texture

Soil is made up of mineral particles of different sizes. Sand particles are the largest. Sand has lots of air space and doesn't compact easily, so water drains quickly out of sandy soil and nutrients are quickly washed away. However, in spring, it is the soil type that will warm most quickly. Clay particles are the smallest and are visible only through a microscope. Water penetrates and drains from clay very slowly. Clay holds the most nutrients, but there is little room for air, so it compacts easily. Clay is the soil that will take the longest time to warm up in spring. Silt particles are smaller than sand particles but larger than clay particles.

The texture of soil is determined by the percentages of sand, silt and clay. Coarse soil is high in sand; fine soil is high in clay. Soil with a balanced mix of the three particle sizes is called loam. A loam soil is the desired soil for any horticultural purposes.

To check the percentages of sand, silt and clay in your soil, place a handful of soil in a clear glass jar and fill it with water. Stir or shake it until all the soil is fully suspended in the water; then set the jar aside to let the soil particles settle out. Sand will settle out first, then silt and finally clay, hopefully into distinct enough layers for easy observation. You can use a ruler to measure the depth of each layer and do some calculations to determine the soil particle percentages, or you can simply look and make a rough estimate of the percentages.

If you are blessed with a soil that is less than perfect, as most of us are, you will need to take steps to improve the soil to ensure your landscape is able to be the best it can be. The most difficult soil to manage is one that is high in clay. However, there is hope—the addition of lots and lots of organic matter over many years will transform this soil into a great horticultural medium.

Soil Structure

Soil structure is the arrangement of the mineral and organic components into stable aggregates. The soil aggregation process is aided by roots pushing through the soil and secreting certain substances, by wetting and drying, by freezing and thawing and especially by soil microorganisms in their search for food.

Coarse soils have large pore spaces; finer soils have fewer large pore spaces but more capillary spaces. Water and air move easily through large pores, whereas water is retained in the smaller pores. The smaller the pore size, the more tightly the water is held in the soil. **Soils with good structure have a balance of large and small pores.** Intense traffic destroys soil structure.

The different types of soil structures include single grain, granular or crumb, platy, blocky, columnar, prismatic and massive. The appearances of the different soil structures are well described by their names. Single grain and granular (crumb) soil structures are the best for growing most plants. Straight sand has a single grain structure that improves as a horticultural soil with the addition of organic matter. Loam usually has a granular- (crumb-) type structure and is the best soil for gardening purposes. The other soil structure types need some amending before planting.

Cation exchange capacity (CEC) is the measure of the ability of a soil to retain nutrients in the form of cations (positively charged atoms or groups of atoms). Some soil components are able to absorb more cations than others. Organic matter and clay have the ability to absorb many cations (a high CEC) as compared to sand, which has a very low CEC.

Organic Matter in Soil

The organic matter in soil is extremely important from a horticultural standpoint. Organic matter includes both living and dead components. The dead components are the residues, metabolites and waste products of plants, animals and microorganisms. The living components are composed of bacteria, fungi, nematodes, protozoa, arthropods and earthworms. These organisms decompose organic compounds, including plant and animal residues and wastes, pesticides and other pollutants. They trap and store nitrogen and other nutrients in their bodies, and they produce hormones that plants use. Their activities enhance soil structure, allowing for better air and water movement into the soil and less runoff. They compete with and prey on plant pests, and they provide food for aboveground animals. **The living soil organisms, the dead organic matter components, the plants and the aboveground animals make up what is known as the soil food web.**

Soil is alive. **In a handful of soil, there is a greater population of organisms than there are people on earth.** Soil scientists have discovered that in a teaspoon of healthy agricultural soil, there are approximately 100 million to 1 billion bacteria, several metres of fungal hyphae, 10,000 to 100,000 protozoa and 10 to 50 beneficial nematodes. There are also 3500 arthropods and 150 to 1000 earthworms per cubic metre of healthy agricultural soil.

Healthy soils with a thriving soil food web are capable of suppressing diseases so that no fungicides, nematicides or bactericides are necessary. If your soil has root-feeding nematodes, it is not a healthy soil.

Mycorrhizal fungi form a symbiotic relationship with plant roots. The fungi help with water and nutrient uptake and protect the roots from fungal diseases. The roots provide the fungi with sugars and other nutrients that the fungi need to thrive. Most plants, especially trees, benefit from this association. Mycorrhizal inoculants are available commercially and are applied at planting time. The mycorrhizal fungi need to be in contact with the plant roots for the relationship to develop. Many mustard family (Brassicaceae) and goosefoot family (Chenoipodiaceae) plants do not form mycorrhizal associations.

Soil pH

The pH of soil is its measure of acidity or alkalinity. A pH of 7 is neutral; higher numbers (up to 14) indicate alkaline conditions, and lower numbers (down to 0) indicate acidic conditions. **Soil pH affects nutrient availability, microorganism activity (neutral soil favours microbial activity) and the solubility of toxic elements.** Although some plants prefer acidic or alkaline soils, many ornamental plants grow best in a mid-range pH between 5.5 and 7.0, with an optimal pH of 6.5.

Soils tend to become acidic in areas where rainfall is plentiful. **A slightly acidic soil pH of 6.5 has the highest availability of plant nutrients.** Strongly acidic soils lead to poor soil structure, low earthworm populations, poor rooting, low plant vigour and a reduction of drought tolerance. They also cause increased thatch accumulation in lawns.

Alkaline soils are common in areas where rainfall is limited and the soils are not leached of excess salts. **Soils with a pH between 7.5 and 8.4 can be detrimental to plant growth.**

Saline soils are not a function of pH but have a high salt content and are often seen with a white crust. The source of this crust can be the irrigation water,

drainage water, groundwater from a high water table or the weathering of the soil parent material. Sodic soils have a pH greater than 8.4, a high sodium content and poor soil structure.

Generally, sodic soils are not suitable to use for gardens or lawns. There are some plant species that have a high tolerance for sodium in soils. They are known as halophytes, or "salt-loving" plants. Wheatgrasses have a high tolerance for sodium in soils.

Saline and sodic soils occur in areas with arid, sunny conditions and where soil drainage is restricted. Some areas in southern Saskatchewan and Alberta are prone to these soils. These areas lack good surface drainage and have low soil permeability.

Get to know the pH of your soil before you begin to select plants. Get a soil test done, and observe the plants that are already growing on your property; they may indicate whether the soil is acidic or alkaline. Changing the pH of soil can take a long time, and it is often better to select plants that are adapted to the soil than to modify the soil.

Drainage

Drainage includes how well the water moves into the soil (infiltration), how well the water moves through the soil (percolation), how well the subsoil drains and how well the surface drains. **Good surface drainage requires that the ground have a minimum 1% slope away from buildings and toward drains.**

The soil's texture and the degree the land slopes influence the drainage properties of your soil. Rocky soil on a hillside will probably drain very quickly and should be reserved for those plants that prefer a very well-drained soil. Low-lying areas retain water longer, and some areas may rarely drain at all. Moist areas suit plants that require a consistent water supply, and areas that stay wet can be used for plants that prefer boggy conditions.

Waterlogged soils can cause shallow rooting, lack of vigour and poor health for plants that need good drainage. Poor aeration, increased disease incidents, risk of damage to soil structure and an increased likelihood of the soil being compacted are other problems associated with waterlogged soils. Wet soils are slow to warm up in spring.

Subsurface drainage may be necessary if your soil lacks good internal drainage. A lack of internal drainage can be caused by poor aeration, compacted soil or clay soil. It is possible that, even though your topsoil drains well enough, it may be sitting on impenetrable clay that does not drain at all.

When there are two different, distinctly textured soils sitting one on top of the other, such as sand over gravel or loam topsoil over a clay subgrade, you have a soil interface that does not allow the free flow of water downward—you have a "perched" water table. Water will not move downward until the entire soil profile above the interface is saturated, and if the subsoil is compacted clay that does not allow water to move through it, you now have a drainage problem. Soil below a perched water table is often dry.

Try this simple drainage test to check how quickly water drains from the soil. Dig a test hole 30 cm (12") in diameter and 30 cm (12") deep. Fill the hole to the top with water and let it drain completely. Fill the hole with water again and note the time. Note the time again when the water has completely drained from the hole. A drainage rate of 1 cm (½") or less per hour is considered poor and may require expensive drainage work to alleviate the problem.

Soil Profile

Soil is usually distributed in horizontal layers known as horizons. A soil profile is the vertical arrangement of those horizons. **The arrangement and composition of horizons in a soil profile allows soil scientists to classify soils.**

The main soil horizons are designated by the capital letters O, A, B, C and E. O is a layer of organic material, such as leaf litter and humus, that sits atop the soil profile. The A horizon is your topsoil layer. The subsoil is designated by the letter B. The C horizon is partially broken up bedrock, also know as regolith. The E horizon is a subsurface horizon that has had most of its minerals and clay leached out to lower layers. Soil horizons may also have a lowercase letter beside the main designation that describes properties or limitations of the horizon.

Dig a hole to expose your soil profile down to 1 m (40"). This allows you to see the depth and composition of the individual horizons, and if the soil is relatively undisturbed or if it has been altered, such as seen in new home construction when the topsoil has been stripped off for construction and replaced when the construction is completed. Some plants require a very deep soil, while other plants thrive in shallower soil.

In an undisturbed soil, or relatively undisturbed soil, the soil microorganisms will also have arranged themselves in horizontal layers, and any disturbance will disrupt the soil microorganism profile. **When digging a hole or trench, always attempt to replace the soil at the depth from which it was removed so as not to overly disturb the soil microorganisms.**

Soil Testing

Two types of soil tests will let you know exactly what is happening in your soil. A standard soil test measures pH level, nutrient content (amount and forms) and how much organic matter is present. **Standard soil tests will provide suggestions on how to alter the soil's characteristics (pH, mineral content, percentage of organic matter) to grow the plants you want to grow.**

The other type of test is a food web assay. This test counts total and active bacteria, total and active fungi, numbers and types of protozoa and numbers and types of nematodes. It also assesses whether the sample is aerobic or anaerobic, identifies the kind and amount of beneficial mycorrhizal colonization on the roots (if you include roots in the sample) and determines how much of the plant surface is covered with microorganisms. **The food web assay will provide suggestions on how to bring the soil life into the balance and diversity needed to grow the plants you want to grow.**

Standard soil tests and food web assays cost relatively little considering the information they provide. Standard soil tests done by accredited labs give more accurate, comprehensive results and better recommendations than the results you will get from do-it-yourself soil-testing kits. Contact the labs for directions on how to take and submit samples. Both standard soil tests and food web assays provide useful information when planning your garden and landscape. **Inform the labs of the plants you intend to grow; the labs can provide specific recommendations on how to best amend the soil to grow those plants.** It may also be the case that your soil would be better to grow plants other than what you have selected. Have the standard soil test done first because it is important that the technicians doing the food web assay know the chemistry of the soil.

Initial Soil Preparation

Soil preparation is the key to establishing a good garden or lawn. **Initial soil preparation can truly be done at any time of the year as long as the soil is not frozen or overly wet or dry.** Gardeners in areas that experience cold winters and mild summers (most of Canada) tend to plant in spring so that the plants are well established before the next cold winter. Complete your initial soil preparation by late summer or early fall, then allow the soil to settle over winter. Gardeners in areas with mild winters and hot summers tend to plant in late summer to early fall so that plants are established before experiencing the next hot summer. Begin your soil preparation in spring to early summer so that the soil has a chance to settle before planting.

Subsoil

Check your soil profile to see what is present under your garden or landscape surface. Dig down to expose the subsoil layer to see if it is compacted or if there are any layers of soil that might interfere with water and air movement in the soil. If the subsoil is compacted or drains poorly, remove all the topsoil and stockpile it. Removing the topsoil provides an opportunity to change the subgrade and ensure that the subsoil is adequately drained.

Adjust the subgrade so that water drains away from the house. The subgrade is the grade of subsoil beneath the topsoil.

Mix in 5–10 cm (2–4") of good-quality compost as deep as possible after you have adjusted the grade. Compost will improve the porosity of the soil and combat compaction.

Relieving and Avoiding Soil Compaction

Compaction—the pressing together of the soil particles into a denser soil mass—is caused by foot and vehicle traffic and rain or irrigation droplets (especially on bare soil). The heaviest compaction occurs in the top 5–8 cm (2–3") of the soil surface. **For areas in your landscape that have constant traffic, consider a raised or paved path.**

New construction methods often severely compact the subsoil around new homes, reducing the amount of pore space, including capillary pores in the soil. Capillary pores, which are the smallest pores, are important because they facilitate the upward movement of moisture between soil particles. Unobstructed capillary pores allow plants to draw water from as deep as possible in the soil.

Compacted soils are often void of plant life other than the plants that do well in compacted soils. Dandelions, knotweed, pineapple weed, field bindweed and quackgrass are often indicators of compacted soil. Also, compacted soils are hard to dig into, and water tends to stand on the surface.

Soil compaction causes the destruction of the soil structure. It reduces the amount of large and small pore spaces in the soil. Toxic gasses can build up in the root zone, infiltration and percolation of water is reduced and surface runoff is increased. Compacted soils prevent roots from penetrating into and through the soil.

Soil compaction is influenced by the soil texture (sand, silt, clay, organic matter), the soil water content, the severity and frequency of pressure applied to the soil and the amount of plant cover. Clay soils are easy to compact, while soils that are mostly sand resist compaction. Soils that contain a good amount of organic matter will also resist compaction quite well. **If your soil is severely compacted, add as much organic matter as you can, preferably in the form of compost.**

The more water a soil has, up to a point, the more easily it is compacted. Most soil compaction occurs in spring, when the soil is usually the wettest. **Make sure the soil has had a chance to thaw and drain before working it in spring.** The freeze/thaw cycle we experience helps alleviate compacted soil. Wet, soupy soil does not compact in the way that moist soil does, but the soil structure is more completely destroyed. Moist soil can pack together in a ball when you pick up a handful. Wet soil does not pack together at all, but rather will flow through your fingers when you pick up a handful.

Severe soil compaction can occur when people drive a vehicle onto a lawn, especially when the soil is moist or wet. Lay down planks or boards to help distribute the vehicle's weight more evenly. **Try to avoid driving on your lawn in early spring or just following a rain, when the soil will easily compact.**

Installing Underground Hardware and Hardscape Features

Once the subsoil has been graded and amended with compost, it is a great time to install retaining walls, patios or sidewalks, any underground irrigation system components and drainage tile, if needed. Installing these features at this time helps alleviate soil settling below your final established grade, especially in drainage and irrigation trench lines. When thinking about the process to follow in the installation of a landscape, it is really only common sense. Start with the grading and amendment process, move to the installation of any hard materials, and at the end you will install the plants, starting with the trees and ending with the smallest annuals.

It may be difficult or impossible to adjust the subgrade of a landscape or garden. **There may be areas that need extra drainage, and drainage tile can be installed.** Round drainage tile is usually installed in a trench

30 cm (12") deep in the subsoil. Ensure the trench is sloped so that the water will flow once it is in the tile. Place 5 cm (2") of pea gravel on the bottom of the trench and lay in the tile. There should be at least 2.5 cm (1") of pea gravel on both sides of the tile. Fill the trench with pea gravel so it is level with the subsoil grade. Landscape fabric is sometimes used to line the trench before the gravel and tile are installed, and some drainage tile has a covering of landscape fabric. Drainage tiles should be a maximum of 8 m (25') apart if more drainage is needed.

When installing drainage tile, you will need a place for the water to drain into, such as a sump or pond. A sump is essentially a deep hole dug into the ground that is filled with gravel. The sump provides a place for the water to collect before draining into the soil surrounding the sump. If your drainage tile terminates to open air, cover the end with a screen to prevent animals from making their home in the tile.

Soil interface problems can be minimized during the placing of the topsoil over the subsoil. Bring in half your topsoil, half of any soil amendments recommended by a soil test and 5–10 cm (2–4") of good quality compost and mix it as deep as possible into the subsoil. Bring in the remaining topsoil, more compost and the other half of any soil amendments and mix that in as deep as possible. If you have installed drainage tile or underground irrigation, ensure you do not tear it up when cultivating. The final grading of the area can now be done.

𝕯 Installing a Water Feature

Many books that explain the detailed process of installing a pond are available, and expert advice is almost always available from independent suppliers as well as nurseries and garden centres that sell pond equipment and

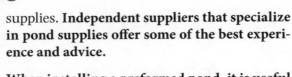

supplies. **Independent suppliers that specialize in pond supplies offer some of the best experience and advice.**

When installing a preformed pond, it is useful to trace the bottom edge to determine the excavation size. Most liners are constructed on two levels. The deepest part of the liner is smaller than the upper half, which contains a plant shelf. Dig the hole just large enough for the deep part of the liner, insert the liner as far as it will go and mark the outside perimeter again. Remove the liner, and dig the hole larger only down to the level of the plant shelf. Any water feature will work better in the long run if the original excavation meets the requirements of the liner. Undisturbed soil is much more supportive and will settle less, thus creating a better base for your liner. The sides and bottom of the hole should be supported with well-packed sand. The entire excavation should be only 5 cm (2") deeper and wider than the pond to allow for the packed sand. Once the liner is in place, wash in the backfill using a garden hose. Level the top edge, and your pond should be ready for plants and fish.

If you are installing a flexible liner, the size of liner that you need is determined after you dig the hole. Use a simple formula to determine the size. Add twice the depth of the pond to the length and width and add 60 cm (2') to each side for finishing the edge.

Metric:

    Liner Width = pond width + (2 x depth) + (2 x 0.60 m)

    Liner Length = pond length + (2 x depth) + (2 x 0.60 m)

For example, if your pond is 1.8 m by 3 m and 60 cm deep, then

Liner Width = 1.8 m + (2 x 0.60 m) + 1.2 m = 4.2 m

Liner Length = 3 m + (2 x 0.60 m) + 1.2 m = 5.4 m

You would need a liner that is 4.2 m by 5.4 m.

Imperial:

Liner Width = pond width + (2 x depth) + (2 x 2')

Liner Length = pond length + (2 x depth) + (2 x 2')

For example, if your pond is 6' by 10' and 2' deep, then

Liner Width = 6' + (2 x 2') + 4' = 14'

Liner Length = 10' + (2 x 2') + 4' = 18'

You would need a liner that is 14' by 18'.

Note: the extra 60 cm (2') will compensate for minor error and will allow some choice for the style of the finished edge.

The actual excavation should be done in the following fashion:

• remove and save the topsoil to use around the pond or elsewhere in your yard

• remove and determine the future use of the subsoil

• level the outside edges of the pond

• shape the walls so they are gently sloped

• dig plant shelves 30 cm (12") deep and wide

• leave a small basin in the bottom to assist in draining the pond; a pump that is placed in this depression will drain all but the last bit of water in the depression, which is easily removed with a pail

• cover the bottom with a few centimetres of sand to protect the liner, and ensure that there are no sharp roots

- lower the liner into the bottom of the hole, work out the wrinkles and pleat the corners

- finish the pond edge in such a way that it shades the liner from UV rays.

Consider safety when adding this type of feature to your landscape. Most water gardens are at least 45 cm (18") deep, which is enough water for a small child to drown in. Electrical outlets should always be properly grounded and hooked up to a circuit breaker. As with any digging done in the landscape, always "dial before you dig."

Grading

Grading is the process of establishing the topography for your garden and landscape and is an important step in minimizing any drainage issues. **Generally, the surface grade should match the subgrade.** You want to ensure that the final grade is smooth, with no ridges, sharp drops or sudden rises. There should be a minimum slope of 1% for surface drainage.

A landscape rake is an excellent tool for doing grade work. The business end of the rake is much wider than a normal garden rake, and the teeth are designed specifically for the purpose of moving soil. Landscape rakes can be expensive to purchase if you are only doing one landscape. Fortunately, tool rental businesses have landscape rakes for rent. When raking, keep the handle of the rake as horizontal as is comfortable for you. Rake in multiple directions. Use the flip side of the rake head to identify and correct humps and hollows. A shovel and spade will also come in handy to fill holes or to shave off high spots.

A sprinkler or irrigation system can be used to identify any humps and hollows during the grading process. Let the soil get wet enough so there is some standing water, which will expose the humps and hollows. Allow the soil to dry, then rake it and roll it. Now is a great time to adjust the heads on your irrigation system to ensure good coverage.

Allow the soil to settle before planting, seeding or sodding. The soil can be settled with a few deep waterings, or with a water-filled roller. The soil will need to be graded again after settling. If the area is for a lawn, you should be able to walk flat-footed on the prepped soil in flat-soled shoes and not leave footprints more than 0.5 cm (¼") deep. If the area is a planting bed, the soil should not be as firmly settled.

Soil Modification

Modifying or amending a soil changes the chemical, biological and physical properties of the soil. **An ideal soil for lawns and gardens is one with good water infiltration and percolation rates, good aeration, a balance of large and small pore spaces for deep rooting, no toxic substances, a healthy soil food web, good cation exchange capacity and good water retention.**

You should know the intended use for the area before you attempt to modify the soil. The different soil amendment materials have different properties and thus different effects on soil texture, soil structure, chemical properties and biological properties. The amendments also have different long-term stability, availability and cost, which is another reason that soil tests are so important. Do not amend your soil without a soil test and a food web assay.

The best time to apply any soil amendment (always based on a soil test) is when the amendments can be incorporated into the soil before planting or seeding.

Texture Amendments

Soils with high clay or sand content are often modi-fied for use in our gardens and landscapes. Gardens with heavier clay and silt soils require much different maintenance than gardens that have sandy soil, and they are often modified to make our maintenance tasks easier. **If you remember only one thing, remember that the addition of organic matter is really the solution to almost any problem soil.**

If your soil is predominantly made up of a very heavy clay, it will take years of modification before you are likely to be happy with the results. **Each spring and fall, add a good amount of organic matter and incor-porate it well.** The larger the organic matter, the bet-ter; you want to retain that organic component for as long as possible. Add some supplemental nitrogen when adding the organic matter to aid in the break-down. One consolation for you if you have a heavy soil: if you stick to adding that organic matter, the final result will be the most beautiful soil.

If you have a very sandy soil, then again, the addition of organic matter will help with the problems associ-ated with too much sand. However, you can remedy this problem in a shorter period of time and again end up with a very nice garden soil.

pH Amendments

Acidic soils lack calcium and magnesium, and phos-phorous is tied up. **Adding lime neutralizes acidic soil and can correct magnesium and calcium deficiencies.** Lime also binds with aluminum and iron in the soil to form soluble compounds that leach from the soil. Alu-minum can be toxic at a low soil pH. Light lime appli-cations on heavily thatched turf can raise the pH of the thatch and stimulate soil microorganisms, which will help to remove the excess thatch. However, too much lime can be detrimental. Alkaline soils with high lime levels may lack the iron needed for healthy growth. Always apply lime, and any other amendment, based on a soil test and food web assay.

There are two forms of lime commonly used. Calcitic limestone is mostly calcium, and dolomitic limestone is composed of both calcium and magnesium. Both forms have a long residual action, and both are faster acting when finely ground. **A soil test will tell you what form of lime is more appropriate for your situation.**

The best time to apply lime is late fall to early winter. The freeze/thaw action in fall and spring helps incorporate the lime into the soil. Liming just before a rainfall is good, too, because the rain washes the lime into the soil.

A good correction for alkaline soil is to apply elemental sulphur, which can be mixed with sand or topdressing for easier application. Do not apply sulphur in summer when plants may be stressed, such as during heat waves or drought periods.

Saline soils can be amended if they can be properly drained. Excess salts can then be leached from the soil. Ensure the irrigation water has a low salt content. Water deeply to help flush the salts from the soil—light, frequent waterings are ineffective. Natural precipitation is good for leaching, provided that drainage is available.

Drainage Amendments

If your soil or subsoil has poor drainage, correct it by adding lots of good-quality compost or compost tea. You can add a soil amendment (based on a soil test), such as calcitic or dolomitic lime. If the subsoil layer is impenetrable and unworkable, or if it is a low area that stays wet, you can install subsurface drainage such as drainage tile.

Some folks think that adding sand to their existing soil will improve the drainage. **We suggest that it is**

unwise to add sand to a clay soil, as concrete may be the result. If you intend to add sand to your soil, do this test first: measure out the appropriate volumes of sand and soil that you would be mixing together in the ground. Mix the soil and sand together in a cardboard box and moisten the entire mixture. Let it dry and check the structure.

It is far better to mix good quality compost into your existing soil rather than try to change the texture. However, you may find that if you increase the organic portion of your soil first and then add a portion of sharp sand, you can avoid the formation of concrete. What makes sand sharp is that the individual particles are spiny, so they do not easily pack. The particles in regular sand are more rounded, so when they are mixed with clay, they pack very easily into an impermeable concrete slab.

University research shows that adding copious amounts of organic matter to clay soil is the best way to turn it into a good growing medium with improved drainage. **If you can add a good 10–15 cm (4–6") of organic matter to your soil and incorporate it well, you will find that the quality improves dramatically.**

Fertility Amendments

Soils often contain all the nutritional requirements for plant growth. However, these elements are often bound to other elements in the soil or are trapped in the bodies of soil microorganisms and are unavailable to the plant. **Enhancing the soil with all kinds of beneficial bacteria, fungi and other microorganisms helps free up the tightly bound elements as the organisms eat and are eaten, releasing nutrients into the soil in forms the plants can use.** Large populations of microorganisms in the soil can trap and use much of the available nutritional elements they need for their growth, which helps reduce nutrients leaching into the groundwater. Enhancing the beneficial soil organism population also helps fight disease and insect attacks and reduces the need for fertilizer and water.

The key to a successful fertility program is to feed the soil, not the plants. Soils are dynamic ecosystems containing many thousands of soil organisms that work in harmony with each other and the plants. Practices such as mixing compost into planting beds, spraying high-quality compost tea on plants or mulching with compost are great for adding life to the soil. Any practice that disrupts the balance of the soil ecosystem, such as the use of pesticides or excessive cultivation, can mean problems for the plants. If you take proper care of your soil, it will produce high-quality plants.

Final Soil Preparation

Prepare your topsoil before you plant to avoid damaging roots later. Control any persistent weeds, remove rocks and other foreign matter, and consider adding a mulch over any exposed soil.

Avoid working your topsoil in spring until it has thawed and dried out a bit. A handful of thawed soil should squeeze into a ball that holds its shape but breaks easily apart when pressed with a thumb or finger.

Topsoil
Some plants do very well with only a thin layer of topsoil, but deeper is better. It is always best to use the soil that exists on site, rather than removing it and importing topsoil. Most soils can be amended to grow most plants. The only reason not to reuse topsoil from a site is if there is something toxic in the soil that can't be alleviated.

For new home construction, you may have to import

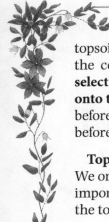

topsoil, and this will often be the topsoil that existed on the construction site before building began. **Always select stone-free, screened topsoil if importing topsoil onto the site.** It is a good idea to have any topsoil tested before purchasing it to reduce potential soil problems before they become part of your landscape.

Topsoil has become a scarce and expensive material. We only have what is present on the planet. When you import topsoil from another site, that site from which the topsoil was taken is degraded.

Weeding

Before planting, seeding or sodding, you will need to control any perennial weeds such as quack grass, creeping harebell, nutsedge and dandelions that have found their way into your soil. It is a good idea to assess the weeds before disturbing the ground so you can decide on the best process of weed removal. However, no method will get rid of all the weeds in an area, including seeds and plants. Some weeds have extensive underground root systems and take time and effort to control. Weeding will always be a yearly maintenance task.

If your soil has a fully functioning soil food web, the soil is less attractive for weed species. Many of the plant species we refer to as weeds are the plants that do best in soils that lack soil life. In nature, it is the job of these pioneer plants to colonize areas that have been disturbed, which helps change the soil for successive plant communities that require a larger and more diverse soil food web.

For more on weeding, see pages 151-54.

Removing Rocks and Debris

Rocks, debris and foreign matter should be removed from as much of the plant root zone as possible, and then removed from the site—do not rebury them.

Plants grown above large, shallow rocks and other buried debris are subject to heat and drought stress because the root depth is limited. Rocks 2.5 cm (1") in diameter and bigger should be removed. Buried debris can damage rototillers and core-aerating machines.

When a stump grinder is used to remove old tree stumps, the stumps should be ground down to a minimum depth of 20 cm (8"); more is better. Any large roots should also be ground down or dug up and removed. Buried wood and stumps will eventually decay, which can lead to air pockets in the soil and depressions in landscape and lawn surfaces. The fungal species that decompose the buried wood may also leave an unacceptable amount of mushrooms on the soil surface.

Mulching

Exposed soil can be displaced by wind, water and traffic. **Consider covering bare soil with mulch or with some kind of crop cover to prevent erosion and to redirect traffic away from the area.** You may have noticed that it is becoming more common to see landscapes that have all exposed soil areas covered by a thick layer of organic mulch. This is a wonderful thing to add to your landscape. A good layer of organic mulch will reduce the evapo-transpiration rate, which will in turn reduce the amount of watering you will need to do to keep your plants happy and reduce the number of annual weeds that germinate. There is also a design component that mulch provides. Especially in a newly planted area, the surface mulch can tie together the property and provide unity.

Any organic material can be used as a surface mulch. Post peelings or wood chips are the least expensive and perhaps the most natural looking. Do not place plastic or landscape fabric underneath the mulch. All those little creatures who live in the soil will break down the

mulch layer and amend your soil with organic matter, but placing a barrier between the mulch and the soil will stop that process from happening. You will have to add to the surface of your mulch every couple of years because it will slowly be incorporated into the soil.

_____

Compost

Compost Basics

Compost is used to add food web organisms to the soil and is also a food source for those organisms. When compost is made correctly, it will contain bacteria, fungi, protozoa, nematodes and often microarthropods. Compost can help add structure elements to soil; it often contains substances such as clay, bits of wood and other fibrous materials that enhance the physical structure and help provide air channels and passages. **Good quality compost adds life to the soil, which improves aeration, water retention, water movement and nutrient availability.**

In forests and meadows, organic debris, such as leaves and other plant bits, breaks down on the soil surface, and the nutrients are gradually made available to the plants growing there. **This process will also take place in your garden beds if you topdress with compost or work the compost into the soil.**

Most organic matter you add to your garden will be of greater benefit if it has been composted first. When the foliage of some plants is allowed to break down naturally, it releases compounds that are toxic to other plants. A compost pile or bin creates a controlled environment where organic matter can be broken down. It is a great way to take care of your household garden waste, which, after composting, will provide you with a quality additive for your garden soil. Composting is most efficient at temperatures of 50–70° C (120–160° F); composting occurs at lower temperatures, but the time

period is much longer. Good composting methods reduce the possibility of spreading pests and diseases.

Compost can modify the pH of soil. Whether the pH is raised or lowered depends on the pH of the soil and compost. In some cases, decaying organic matter releases acids and can help lower the pH in alkaline soils. The addition of compost will also buffer the soil to resist any sudden or large changes in the pH.

Compost contains microorganisms and micronutrients that are often not present in commercial synthetic fertilizers. It is a great additive for any soil, with the only problem being never having as much compost as you need!

Qualities of Good Compost

All composts are not the same. **Properly made compost will not have weed seeds, human pathogens or heavy metals in detectable levels.** The following list provides some of the characteristics of good-quality compost and things to be aware of about compost.

Compost should have:

- a light, crumbly texture with no visible or identifiable debris, such as pieces of wood, and should look like dark brown topsoil.

- an earthy, mushroomy aroma. Do not purchase or use compost that has any funny or foul odour.

- an ash content less than 30%, with better compost containing less ash.

- a carbon to nitrogen ratio of 30:1 (C:N) or less. The more carbon present in the compost, the more nitrogen is tied up in the decomposition process.

- a pH of 6.0–7.5. A pH of 6.5–7.0 is an ideal range for most plants.

- very few (if any) weed seeds. If possible, it is a good idea to visit the location where the compost is made to see if there is an abundance of weeds there.

- a 30–50% moisture content so that it is easy to work with and mixes well into soil. Compost with greater than 60% moisture content is heavy, hard to handle and tends to clump when you try to mix it into the soil. Compost with less than 20% moisture content floats on top of the soil when trying to incorporate it, blows away easily in a medium to stiff wind (which can leave a dust film on cars, houses, plants, etc.) and may get into your eyes and lungs when using it.

Check to ensure that the types and amounts of metal in the compost are below health guidelines.

Check for salt content and type of salt; some salts are more damaging than others (i.e., sodium) and some plants are more sensitive to some forms of salts. Compost with a high salt concentration can be leached with fresh water immediately after application. Salt-heavy compost does more damage when surface applied than when incorporated.

Getting Your Compost Started

Compost can be made in a pile, in a wooden box or in a purchased composter bin anytime, anywhere. It can be made above ground in boxes, barrels, piles, cages, garbage cans or mounded rows. It can be made below ground in pits, trenches and holes. It can also be made inside your house, on a balcony, deck, patio or in the garage. If you do not wish to make your own compost, it can be purchased from most garden centres. Many municipalities now recycle yard wastes into compost

that is made available to residents. Contact your city hall to see if this valuable resource is available to you. However, composting is not a complicated process. A pile of kitchen scraps, grass clippings and fall leaves will eventually break down if simply left alone.

Procrastinators beware. **There is no excuse not to start a composter, since it can be started at any time of year.** It doesn't matter what temperature it is, or season, nor does it matter how much you have to start with. A small compost bin or heap can always be made larger, and your skills will build over time, resulting in a superior product useful both indoors and out.

Location

When choosing a location for your bin, there are several things to look for. Choose carefully because your location should remain a permanent one.

- Consider locations with good drainage so that the liquid from the mixture can drain away freely (unless you have an enclosed bin, in which case the liquid collected can later be used to sprinkle over your plants).

- A sheltered or protected location is also preferred—you don't want your bin to lose its contents in a storm, and if you live in an area that experiences frequent rain, some form of cover will prevent the compost from becoming waterlogged and the nutrients from being leached away through run-off.

- Choose a location with level ground, or level the spot where you plan to put a composter.

- A sunny location is helpful to most commercial bins, assisting in the heat necessary to cook off any pathogens, while expediting the process as well.

- A shady spot is better for most wood and wire bins, which are prone to drying out in locations that are too hot, sunny and windy.

- Open compost piles are best in sunny locations.

Avoid putting your composter too close to a tree or directly under a downspout or eavestrough. Tree roots are known to take the nutrients from the pile of compost itself, which defeats the entire purpose, if you plan on spreading nutrient-filled compost elsewhere in your garden. Locations that are directly under downspouts and eavestroughs will become too wet. The excess water will also leach out most of the nutrients, diluting the best elements from your compost.

The soil that the composter is placed upon is full of decomposer organisms that inevitably travel up into the compost. **A location atop soil is always best rather than one on concrete or any other hard surface.** This rule does not apply to worm bins and the like. They're meant to be sealed and not in contact with the soil.

Convenience is an important factor when choosing a location for your composter. How far do you want to travel with your food scraps? Are you going to have to trudge through the snow to get to your composter in winter? Ease of access is paramount so that you can actually get to the compost when you want it.

Some people prefer to hide their composter from view, but keeping it in plain sight can encourage discussion, and you'll find yourself discussing techniques with neighbours, friends and family. Just keep it away from your neighbours' patios, decks and areas where they're apt to entertain. They may not want to discuss your compost practices at their next outdoor dinner party.

Method

Choose a method of composting that will become part of your regular routine. Many methods of composting exist, and some require more of your time and attention than others. Each method offers a different range of how much time and attention it will require.

Decide what type of materials you have at your disposal, why you want to begin composting, how much time you have, how tidy the location has to be and how much money you would like to spend. If you have only a small space and little time, a commercial container or bin may be best. If space and time aren't an issue, then a handmade, three-tier bin might be more apropos. The choice is yours.

If you have limited space, consider the simple process of worm composting. A plastic container with drainage and air holes, a layer of shredded, moistened newspaper (avoid glossy newsprint) and some red worms, along with your kitchen scraps (minus any meat products), will give you black, nutrient-rich worm castings in as few as six weeks. See pages 80-84 for more detail about worm composting.

Passive, or cool, composting may take one to two seasons for all the materials to break down. An active, or hot, compost pile shortens the composting time considerably.

☞ Active Composting

Use dry as well as fresh materials, with a higher proportion of dry, high-carbon content materials than fresh, green matter. Appropriate dry matter includes chopped straw, shredded leaves and sawdust. Green matter may consist of kitchen scraps, grass clippings and pulled weeds. The green matter breaks down quickly and produces nitrogen, which composting organisms use to break down dry matter.

Arrange your compost pile in layers. Start with a layer of dry material, add a layer of green material, add a thin layer of garden soil or previously finished compost to introduce beneficial soil microorganisms, then repeat the layering until the pile is about 1.2 m (4') tall and wide. It is also acceptable to toss all the materials into the bin and stir them up.

Ensure your compost pile stays moist. The compost should be moist but not soaked—about as wet as a wrung-out sponge. As you are building the pile, you can sprinkle water between the layers. Some compost bins have lids that exclude rainwater, so you will have to provide water when necessary, or leave the lid off on a rainy day.

Adding nitrogen, such as that found in fertilizer, will speed up decomposition. Avoid strong concentrations of nitrogen, or you may kill beneficial organisms.

Turn the pile over or poke holes in it with a pitchfork every week or two. Air must get into the pile in order to speed up decomposition.

A well-aerated compost pile generates a lot of heat, reaching temperatures up to 70° C (160° F). At this high temperature, weed seeds are destroyed and many damaging soil organisms are killed. Most beneficial organisms will not be killed unless the temperature exceeds 70° C. To monitor the temperature of the compost near the middle of the pile, you will need a thermometer that is attached to a long probe, similar to a large meat thermometer. Turn your compost once the temperature drops. Turning and aerating the pile will stimulate the process to heat up again.

When you can no longer recognize the matter that you put into the compost bin, and the temperature no longer rises upon turning, your compost is ready to be mixed into your garden beds. The process may take as little as one month.

☙ Passive Composting

Making a passive compost pile involves simply dumping yard waste into a pile. This material may include weeds pulled from the garden, pruned branches cut into small pieces, grass clippings, fall leaves and fruit and vegetable scraps. Never compost meat scraps.

Passive compost piles may take a season or two to break down into compost. **The passive pile will have a layer of pure black gold at the bottom that looks much like the leaf mould found in the woods.**

Compost Materials

Dry, High-Carbon Materials

Keep a supply of dry, high-carbon content materials, such as shredded leaves or chopped twigs and branches, near your compost bin to cover the fresh green layer. Some gardeners will collect leaves from their neighbours' yards or pinch bags of leaves left for the garbage collectors to add to their leaf supply.

Straw and hay are a good source of dry, high-carbon material if there is limited access to leaves. Active composting is best for hay and straw to destroy any weed seeds.

You can add shredded newspaper and computer paper to your compost pile. Paper shredding is a common practice these days, and the shredded paper is another source of dry, high-carbon material.

Any material you add to a compost bin will break down faster if the material is chopped or shredded to increase the surface area that is exposed to the organisms that break down the material. Mulching lawn mowers work great for shredding leaves and twigs. Sharpen the blade after you have completed the shredding process.

Green Materials

When adding grass clippings to the compost pile, make sure to add only thin layers up to 10 cm (4"), or mix them with your dry, high-carbon content materials before putting them in the bin. Grass clippings are a great source of nitrogen, but they can start smelling bad if the grass layer is too thick.

If you add grass clippings that have pesticide residue, you run the risk of having that pesticide remaining active if you do not allow the compost to completely finish. Avoid adding grass clippings with pesticide residue to your compost pile if you are going to use the compost on edible plants.

Gardeners who live near large bodies of water can collect and add seaweed, lake weeds and algae to their compost piles. Rinse off any salt water before adding the seaweed to the composter.

Composting kitchen scraps can help reduce pressure on the local landfills while providing you with fertilizer for your garden. Many households produce well over 45 kg (100 lb) of kitchen scraps each year. Do not include any meat or dairy products in your compost pile.

Used coffee grounds are excellent to add to your compost pile, or to use as mulch around plants, especially acid-loving plants. You can toss shredded coffee filters into the compost pile, but you should remove the filters if you're using the coffee grounds for mulch.

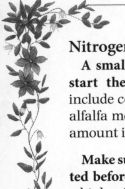

Nitrogen Sources

A small amount of nitrogen is often used to jump-start the composting process. Sources of nitrogen include commercial fertilizers, bone meal, blood meal, alfalfa meal and aged livestock manure. Only a small amount is needed to be effective.

Make sure all livestock manure is thoroughly composted before using it in the garden. Some manures have a high nitrogen or salt content and can easily burn plants. Active composting is best if you're adding manure to your compost pile because the high temperatures will destroy the weed seeds present in the manure.

Avoid adding dog or cat poo to your compost because these substances may contain disease-causing organisms—no kitty litter either.

Ash

Small amounts of wood ash can be used in your compost pile or bin. Ash is alkaline, and it is a good addition when composting conifer needles, oak leaves and other acidic materials. Avoid ash from coal and charcoal because it may contain elements toxic to plants.

Maintaining Your Compost Pile

General Maintenance

A good size for a compost pile is 1–1.2 m (3–4') tall and wide. This size allows water and air to reach every part of the pile, and the pile will retain the heat necessary for breaking down the raw compost materials.

Compost decomposes most quickly when there is a balance between dry and fresh materials. There should be more dry matter, such as chopped straw or shredded leaves, than green matter, such as vegetable scraps and grass clippings. Try to maintain a balance year-round.

Excessive dry material will compost slowly, while too much green material can create a smelly compost bin.

Layering dry and green matter, along with a little garden soil or previously finished compost, will introduce decomposer organisms to your compost, enabling the decomposition process to begin.

Kitchen scraps in the compost bin tend to attract insects and other local wildlife. **Bury kitchen scraps deep inside the pile to reduce unwanted scavenging.**

Avoid putting weed seeds and diseased or pest-ridden plants into your compost pile, or you risk spreading problems throughout your garden.

Compost won't decompose properly if it is too wet or too dry. Keep the pile covered during heavy rain and sprinkle it with water if it is too dry. The correct level of moisture can best be described as that of a wrung-out sponge.

To aerate the compost pile, use a garden fork to poke holes in it or turn it regularly. Use a thermometer with a long probe attached, similar to a large meat thermometer, to check the temperature in your pile. When the temperature reaches 70° C (160° F), give the pile a turn.

Your compost pile will shrink as the raw materials are broken down. **Add material on top or move the finished compost to a storage spot and begin again.**

Elders are the ideal companion to plant close to a compost bin because worms love the leaves that fall to the ground. Elders attract worms, and worms are gold for a compost heap.

You can hide your compost pile by growing tall plants around it. Annuals such as sunflowers work well, especially with the extra nutrition available adjacent to the compost pile.

Winter Maintenance

Don't let cold temperatures and winter prevent you from composting. Decomposition will slow down in winter, and the mound may even freeze solid, but you should continue to add scraps to the pile because the freeze/thaw cycle will break down the cellular structure of the added materials. Keep a bag or basket of leaves from fall to cover up food scraps in the winter months.

If you start your composter in fall, it's helpful to keep it as active as possible during winter. By simply adding nitrogen-rich scraps into the heap under layers of organic insulation, the process will be accelerated, and the insulation will help keep the heat inside the pile. Pull up faded annuals and vegetable plants and shred them before adding them to the compost pile in fall.

If your compost bin is outdoors and directly on the ground with an open bottom, it's helpful to dig a hole in the centre 15–30 cm (6–12") deep, which helps keep the heat in while building the pile of compost and materials higher. This hole is particularly helpful in the winter months.

Don't bother to aerate your compost in winter unless it begins to smell bad. Turning the compost at this point will only allow the heat to escape.

Using Your Compost

Finished compost is dark in colour and light in texture and should smell like rich, mushroomy soil. **When you can no longer recognize what went into the compost, it is ready for use.** Access the finished compost by moving the top of the pile aside.

When adding compost to your garden, simply spread it on the surface. You can also work the compost into the soil a few centimetres; the majority of plant feeder roots are within 15 cm (6") of the soil surface.

Incorporate compost into a new planting bed at least one month prior to planting to allow the soil to stabilize.

The best time to spread compost onto annual flower beds and vegetable gardens is in fall when the plants are done and removed. The soil organisms will incorporate most of the compost into the soil by springtime. Snow melt and spring rains will help move nutrients down into the soil. Topdress lawns with 0.5–1 cm (¼–½") of compost in fall.

Mulch around trees, shrubs, perennials, vegetable gardens and annual plantings with 2.5–5 cm (1–2") of compost in spring. To reduce the chance of stem rot, do not allow the compost to be within 2.5 cm (1") of the stems.

Mix up to half the volume of your container of potting soil with high-quality compost, especially when growing heavy-feeding plants.

If your compost supply is limited, use it first in areas that need it most, such as your vegetable garden or prized flower bed. Or, just add a trowelful to each planting hole.

Use your compost to make compost tea to water around, or to spray on, your plants as a foliar feed.

Compost finishes faster and breaks down quicker in the garden in warm, moist climates. **Gardeners in these areas will need to add compost on a more regular basis than gardeners in colder, drier climates.**

Worm Composting

If you're unable to compost outdoors for any reason, but particularly if you live in an apartment or condo, then worm composting is for you. It's not as gross as it sounds, and it will allow you to compost all kitchen waste, rather than simply throwing it away.

Worm composting, also known as vermicomposting, is simply a process of breaking down organic matter with worms *and* microorganisms. **Many municipalities offer a course in worm composting, and if you can't find one locally, then search online, at your library or at your local bookstore for resources.**

There are many advantages to worm composting, and reducing waste that might otherwise go into the landfill is just one. It takes up little room and requires little of your time and resources. An appropriate container, a little newspaper, water, kitchen scraps and a few thousand worms are all you need to get started.

Worm castings are one of the most invaluable compost materials available. They are highly valued because of their water retention capacity, nutrient content and ease of use. **Worm compost and castings are the perfect amendment to potting soil, garden beds and the lawn.**

Setting Up Your Worm Composter

Worm composting can be done either indoors or outdoors on a balcony or porch. If your region always stays above 5° C (40° F), the composter can stay outdoors year-round; however, in most of Canada, it will have to be brought indoors when fall or winter approaches or when the temperature drops below 5° C. Ensure that you have a space indoors for the composter if it is only outdoors seasonally.

Indoors, you will require an out-of-the-way location for your worm composter. Make sure it's easily accessible by you but not by your pets. Select a location that isn't too hot; in the basement or a cupboard or even under a table or on a shelf are suitable placements.

Determine what size of bin to use to house the worms, bedding and scraps. It should be approximately 20–30 cm (8–12") deep. Any deeper, and the bottom layers of material could become anaerobic and smelly. A great guideline to determine how much length and width you need uses imperial measurements: one square foot of surface area per pound of weekly garbage. In other words, a bin that is 2' x 3' on top and 1' deep would be ideal for a family that produces 6 lb of food waste weekly, or a family of four to six people. A bin that is 2' x 2' on top and 1' deep will suffice for two to three people, and a bin that is 1.5' x 2' on top and 1' deep is ideal for one to two people in the household. Weigh your food waste in advance to determine what size of bin would be best for you.

A plastic container is useful for worm composting, as long as you add air holes prior to adding the worms. Plans for building wooden composters are available online and at your local environmental centre or association that offers composting courses. **It's best that your container have a lid to keep curious creatures out and to keep the worms' environment dark and moist.** Don't worry about the worms getting out; they are shy creatures and are keen to stay where it's dark, moist and where they're fed regularly.

Once you have your container ready, you'll need bedding material for the worms. Good bedding holds moisture and allows for air circulation. This environment will provide a place for the worms to live and work. **Bedding can be made out of a variety of materials including straw, peat moss, leaves, corrugated cardboard or paper and soil.** Shredded newspapers make great bedding, mixed with a little soil. Avoid any coloured newspapers because the ink can contain

heavy metals, which will cause harm to the worms and the garden where the compost will inevitably end up.

Moisten whichever bedding material you decide to use. Immerse newspaper in water for a few minutes, then give it a good wringing out. Cut it into 2.5–5 cm (1–2") strips and add the strips to the bin. Fluff them up if they begin to clump or become compacted. Corrugated cardboard can also be immersed in water, wrung out and shredded. Peat moss can be used as an alternative, but you'll have to add water to the peat moss to get it moist, along with a small quantity of crushed egg shells to counter the acidity of the peat.

Layer the bedding to a depth of approximately 7–10 cm (3–4") or until the bin is about half full. Add a 5 cm (2") layer of soil, dead leaves, straw, peat moss or any combination of these materials. It's important to add materials that have never been in contact with pesticides, herbicides or any type of toxic chemical. Mist, sprinkle or spray the bedding until it's damp, but not soaked or dripping. It should be as moist as a wrung-out sponge. The bedding should be in balance with the worms' moisture content, which is approximately 75%, and once you get started, the kitchen scraps should keep the composter moist enough for the worms to live and work.

Now, bring on the worms. **Red worms, also known as red wigglers, or African night crawlers are the two types of worms to look for.** Red worms produce well in temperatures of 20–25° C (68–77° F). They cannot survive outside in winter unless the compost container is well insulated, and even then, there's a risk of the worms perishing from the cold. African night crawlers can tolerate temperatures of 20–26° C (68–79° F), but ideally, 24° C (75° F) is best. This type of worm cannot survive below 15° C (60° F), and growth and reproductive rates drop when temperatures drop below 20° C (68° F).

Worms can be purchased from a few sources. Most large municipalities have a compost program available, and they often offer worms for sale. Some municipalities have an environmental resource centre offering courses on composting, and they will have worms for sale as well. Garden centres sometimes carry worms, or they may offer a special order service to bring them in, as will bait suppliers. If you can't find a supplier locally, call your provincial recycling council, local agricultural college or browse the web and environmentally themed magazines and stores.

Feeding Your Worms

Feed your worms regularly, but be careful what you provide as food. The same rules apply to all forms of composting: no meat, bones, fish scraps or fatty items such as butter or other dairy. Basically, if it came from an animal, it does not belong in the bin.

Worms can plough through almost anything, including coffee grounds and the filter, tea bags, finely ground egg shells, vegetable and fruit scraps, bread and baked goods, rice and grains, nuts and pasta. **Ensure that everything is finely chopped or ground up, enabling the worms to break your scraps down easier and quicker than they would in large pieces or chunks.**

You can make a "milkshake" of sorts for your worm bin by putting your scraps into a blender, along with a bit of water. Blend the scraps into a puree and pour the mix into the bin for the worms to consume, speeding the process along exponentially.

Some scraps, regardless of how small you cut them up, will take longer to decompose than others—citrus peels, for example. It can take up to a month for certain scraps to break down, but they will eventually. Just give them time.

Egg shells should be let to dry out completely before crushing them into fine bits in a paper bag. Otherwise, the "skin" inside of the brittle outer shell will make crushing the shell more difficult.

Kitchen scraps and food waste are ideal feed for your worms but should always be covered with the bedding material to discourage an infiltration of fruit flies.

General Care and Maintenance

Worms, like every other living creature, have certain needs that must be met in order for them to remain healthy.

- The best range of temperature for worm composting is 20–25° C (68–77° F).

- Moisture is imperative for the worms in order for them to breathe through their skin, but too much moisture will cause them to suffocate. Learn how to find the right balance.

- Worms need oxygen, so air circulation in the container or bin is important to maintain.

- Worms prefer a neutral pH, approximately 7.0 in the scheme of things. Anything below 5.5 will cause them to die off. Balance acidic food scraps, such as citrus peels, with pulverized egg shells, which are alkaline.

If your worm population begins to outgrow its container, start a second bin or share some of your worms with friends and family. If they don't have a worm composter of their own, then maybe it's time to help them set one up, with a contribution from you. You could also give some of the worms to a school, so it can start a vermicomposting project for the kids to learn about the process. Even if you give away half of your worms, the population will continue to grow over time, as long as they're being fed and housed. If you can't find anyone to take some of your worms, you can leave the population alone, and it will begin to stabilize itself based on space and food allotment without overtaking your bin.

If your worm population is decreasing rather than increasing, the likely culprit is a bin that is too hot. High temperature can adversely affect your worm bin and its population. Discontinue feeding the worms for approximately one week if that is the case.

Excessive moisture is also a killer, as is high acidity or bedding that needs replacing.

Believe it or not, you can overfeed your worms. Grey mould is the most common indicator of too much food. It's simply that the worms can't keep up with the intake. **If your bin gets grey mould, remove the lid from the bin, allowing the mould to dry out, and discontinue feeding your worms for at least a week so they can catch up.**

If you are sensitive to moulds, then a worm bin may not be right for your household. Vermicomposting does not produce the heat necessary to kill off pathogens, which won't be a problem if you've omitted meat and diseased material from your bin. However, moulds will always be present at some level.

To protect your worms from predators outdoors, be sure to use a lid. Otherwise, critters such as birds, toads, snakes, slugs, beetles, leeches, hedgehogs, moles and foxes may find your bin a virtual buffet.

If You Get Fruit Flies...

Worm composters are sometimes a haven for fruit flies and fungus gnats. It will depend on the amount of fruit scraps that are added to the bin, along with general maintenance of the bin and its contents. Keep in mind that the flies and gnats are not harmful to you, the worms, your bin or anything else, including pets,

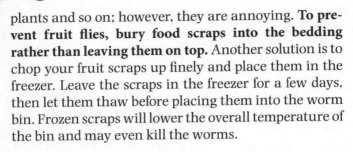

plants and so on; however, they are annoying. **To prevent fruit flies, bury food scraps into the bedding rather than leaving them on top.** Another solution is to chop your fruit scraps up finely and place them in the freezer. Leave the scraps in the freezer for a few days, then let them thaw before placing them into the worm bin. Frozen scraps will lower the overall temperature of the bin and may even kill the worms.

Fruit fly traps are easy enough to construct. Pour 2.5–5 cm (1–2") of beer into a glass. In a piece of plastic, poke a small hole, but make it large enough for the flies to get through. The plastic should be large enough to cover the mouth of the glass with enough allowance to flow over the edge. Secure the plastic in place with a good seal, either with a rubber band or a piece of tape. The flies will be drawn into the glass through the hole to get to the beer, get trapped and die. Vacuuming the flies up in areas where they seem to congregate will help when populations are high, but make sure to dispose of the vacuum bag once you're done, or they'll continue to multiply in the bag as they do in your home.

During the warm months, keep your worm composter outside to keep the populations of fruit flies and fungus gnats out rather than indoors.

If It Smells...

If everything is working as it should, your worm composter shouldn't produce any foul odours; however, if you overload your worm bin with too much water or food, it may begin to stink. Stop adding food scraps, and the smell should dissipate or disappear in a week or so.

A smelly worm bin may be a sign of a lack of oxygen, which is often connected to too much moisture, but it's easy to correct. Simply fluff up the bedding materials and compost, integrating oxygen into the mix. Turn the material over so the bottom layer can dry out a little.

If a smell is still emanating from your bin, check for standing water at the bottom. Water should never be allowed to collect. Drain it out and add more holes to the bottom of the bin for additional drainage, reducing the likelihood of a stinky bin.

An easy way to determine if your bin is too wet is by monitoring the items you add to your bin. If you're adding food scraps but no extra water, then it's very likely that your bin is not suffering from being too wet. However if the material in your bin seems wetter than a squeezed-out sponge, it will begin to produce a foul odour. This can be corrected by turning the material in the bin more often to dry it out. Adding fresh new bedding will also help to counteract the moisture, putting things back into balance.

Acidity can also cause your bin to smell, especially if you've added a lot of acidic material such as tomatoes, citrus fruits and so on. A soil test kit will help you determine acidity levels, as would litmus paper. Generally, the ideal pH level in a worm bin is neutral to slightly acidic, which is approximately 6–7. By adding 1–2 tablespoons of powdered egg shells to the mix each week, you can counteract the acidity, bringing balance to your bin and eliminating the smell.

Lastly, if a foul odour has formed in your bin, the container itself may be too deep. The materials in a composter will compact somewhat, and if the container is too deep, the compaction becomes too great, eliminating adequate air circulation and oxygen exchange. If you're producing a lot of kitchen waste, then you might want to consider having two shallow bins rather than one deep one.

Harvesting Your Worm Compost

Harvesting times for the finished compost from your bin may differ from other bins. The time it takes for your compost to finish is dependent on a few factors,

including what went into the bin, the quantity of worms, temperature, bedding and moisture content, just to name a few. The average amount of time it takes to complete the cycle is roughly two to three months, from start to finish. However, it may take longer based on the previous factors. You may notice only a drop in the volume of the materials you added over that two- to three-month period, but it is well on its way to a fine end result.

One method of harvesting the finished compost and castings is to start by taking the lid off the container or bin. The worms exposed to light will begin to burrow down lower into the bedding. Scoop out a layer of the finished compost. Place any worms that may have been scooped out along with the compost back into the bin. Put any recognizable scraps to the side as well. Put the finished compost and castings in another container. Wait a minute or two before scooping out more of the finished product, allowing the worms to move farther down. Continue to follow this procedure of removing the compost until you've pretty much reached the bottom, where there will be little else but a mass of worms. Gently dump the worms onto a sheet of plastic or into another container while you prepare a new combination of bedding and salvaged scraps. Replace the worms into the bedding and start the whole process as before.

A second method is to move the composted material back and forth from one side of the bin to another. This should take place when the original bedding is no longer recognizable. Simply move the compost to one side and the worms to the other, and remove the compost. Add new bedding to the empty side of the bin. Bury new food scraps into the new bedding, then cover the bin with a lid. The worms will naturally migrate over to the new mixture where the food is. Once they've moved over, which will take an average of two months, the worms can be exposed to light once again, forcing them into the bottom so the finished product can be scooped out. The compost can be used in your planters and garden.

Worm casting tea is very easy to prepare. Simply take some compost and castings and place them into the centre of a sheet of muslin. Tie the corners of the muslin together to create a "tea bag." Steep the tea bag in a container of water. Ideally, you want one part compost/castings to three parts water. Left overnight or longer, the microorganisms, nutrients and other goodies will build as a concentrate into the water. The end result is a natural liquid fertilizer suitable for use when feeding any of your plants. It's best when diluted a little, which will stretch a batch out for quite some time. If your kitchen scraps are 100% organic, then your compost tea will be too.

Kids and Composting

Get the kids involved by keeping a garbage log. A garbage log will help keep track of your trash and is a fun way to teach your kids about environmental awareness. This simple record sheet can be put on the fridge for ease of access. It basically serves as a garbage inventory. Simply create a column for recyclable items such as paper, kitchen scraps, cans, bottles and plastic and another for any items that will end up in the landfill. The goal is to have more items in the recyclable column and few to none in the landfill column. Reward anyone who makes an effort to recycle and compost.

Kids can also have their own mini compost pile to tend to, if space is available. They'll find it interesting to learn about decomposition and how the whole process works if they have a mini pile of their own to be responsible for. They'll see just how scraps break down, what is needed to make it work and how the end result can be used in the garden.

The mini pile can be outdoors in a small compost bin of their own, or a smaller version can be created in a large glass jar. Simply add layers of material just as you would in a larger version: a few dead leaves as the first layer, followed by a bit of garden soil, a scoop of kitchen scraps, a few more leaves and a thin layer of grass clippings. Top it off with a touch more soil and there you have it, a mini composter. Continue layering until the large jar is full. Add a bit of water with a mister bottle if most of the components are dry as they're going into the jar. A few small twigs can be poked into the mix to allow for adequate air circulation and stability.

Then, experiment! Place the jar in a sunny window or a warm location for a few days or more. Try a shaded or cooler location. Find dry locations as well as damp locations to see what happens. **The perfect location will be the one where the decomposition begins and the materials begin to fall and settle.** Your kids will often see daily changes and will soon learn how the whole process of composting takes place, while learning a valuable lesson about the importance of composting as well.

Selecting and Starting Plants

Planting is the fun part, but in order to do any planting, you must have some plants. Many gardeners consider the trip to the local garden centre to choose their plants an important rite of spring. Others consider starting their own plants from seed one of the most rewarding aspects of gardening. Both methods have benefits, and many gardeners use a combination of the two.

Purchasing Plants

Nurseries and garden centres are excellent resources for help with selecting and growing plants for your garden and landscape. Staff on hand should be willing and able to answer questions, make recommendations and assist you with whatever you need. Any reputable garden centre should have a good selection of popular and reliable plants. Finding unusual specimens could require a few phone calls or a trip to a specialized nursery. Mail-order nurseries can be a great source of new and unusual plants; however, the plants might not be as well adapted to your garden climate as they are to the climate the nursery is in. Locally grown and raised plants often do better than plants grown and raised in other climates.

Go to the garden centre in early spring, earlier than you usually go. Often, uncommon plants are available early, and you may be able to purchase woody plants while they are still dormant. Many garden centres will take your name and call you when the plants you are looking for arrive.

Visit early during the day or very early in the season to ask questions. Weekends and evenings in spring are often very busy, and staff may not have as much time to assist you as they would during slower times. Visits during busy times are better spent purchasing the things you've already decided on.

Ask lots of questions about the plants you are being shown and be prepared to answer any questions asked of you about your garden. Knowing what is needed for specific areas, as well as the climatic conditions and microclimates of your garden, will guide your purchases and ensure that what you purchase will survive. Being able to share the pertinent information about the specific conditions of your site will allow the garden centre professional to do his/her job more efficiently.

Take everything you need to the garden centre. A photo of your house and garden, or even a roughly drawn schematic of your yard, can help garden centre staff make better suggestions for your garden.

Go to the garden centre with some specific ideas (or at least a general idea) of what you want. If you have done a good job of your plan, then you will already know what specific criteria you are looking for. The more vague you are, the more time it will take for the staff to assist you—and the less satisfaction you will likely experience.

Try to follow your plan when shopping for plants; however, it is important to be open to suggestions. The exact plant you are looking for might not be available, but an experienced professional can give you some alternatives that will thrive in that environment and provide the benefits you desire.

Remember to think about all those factors you considered in the planning of the garden, including your

maintenance requirements. Some plants require more maintenance than others. Research the plants you are considering purchasing to ensure that you know the cultural requirements, and compare that to your site criteria.

Choose healthy plants that have been developed for their resistance to common problems and that will perform well in the conditions provided by your garden. The majority of plants chosen should be able to easily survive your climatic conditions. This does not mean that you should not take the liberty to try to grow some things that push the seasonal limitations, but limit those choices to help avoid disappointment with the overall landscape. Beginner gardeners are wise to choose "bullet-proof" plants, such as annual geranium, speedwell or shrubs such as red-twigged dogwood. Remember that by creating specific micro-climates, you can successfully grow a greater variety of plants.

Choose plants that will add landscape value. For example, viburnums are very hardy shrubs that have a spring bloom, great fall colour and often fruit as well, which lasts into those long winter months. They are attractive year-round. And, if strategically planted, they can provide a windscreen beside an outdoor seating area.

Try to choose your plants first for the function or role they will serve in the landscape. For instance, if you are choosing a shade tree for your patio, you need to determine what size the tree would have to be to provide shade. Once you have that information, you can begin looking at hardy trees that will work. Your choice is now narrowed down a little bit, and you can concentrate on the other features that will help to add more value to your landscape.

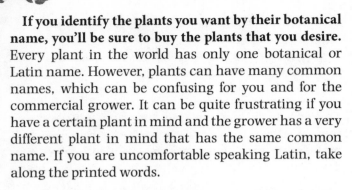

If you identify the plants you want by their botanical name, you'll be sure to buy the plants that you desire. Every plant in the world has only one botanical or Latin name. However, plants can have many common names, which can be confusing for you and for the commercial grower. It can be quite frustrating if you have a certain plant in mind and the grower has a very different plant in mind that has the same common name. If you are uncomfortable speaking Latin, take along the printed words.

Take advantage of end-of-season sales. Many garden centres get rid of woody ornamentals and perennials at reduced prices. You can plant right up until the ground freezes.

Selecting Trees and Shrubs

Many garden centres and nurseries offer a one-year warranty on trees and shrubs. **Always choose the healthiest plants.** Never purchase weak, damaged or diseased plants, even if they cost less. Examine the bark and avoid plants with visible damage. Check that the growth is even and appropriate for the species. Most shrubs should be bushy and branched right to the ground, and most trees should have a strong leader. Observe the leaf and flower buds. If they are dry and fall off easily, the plant has been deprived of moisture. The stem or stems should be strong, supple and unbroken. The root ball should be soft and moist to the touch. Do not buy a plant with a dry root ball.

Woody plants are available for purchase in three forms: bare-root, balled-and-burlapped and container-grown.

Bare-root stock has roots surrounded only by moist sawdust or peat moss and a plastic wrapping. **Reject stock that appears to have dried out during shipping. Keep the roots moist and cool, and plant as soon as possible in spring. Plant your bare-root stock in a large**

container of potting soil if it cannot be planted in the ground immediately.

Balled-and-burlapped (B&B) stock comes with the roots surrounded by soil and wrapped in burlap, often secured with a wire cage for larger plants. The plants are usually field grown and then dug up, balled and burlapped the year they are sold. Large trees are available in this form. The advantage of B&B stock is that it is easier for you to match the soil type the plant was previously grown in to ensure no inhibition of future water patterns. However, the disadvantage of B&B plants is that often many of the roots have been severed, necessitating careful care after transplanting. **Be aware that the soil and root ball can be very heavy, and extra expenses for delivery and planting may apply. It is essential that the root ball remains moist. You can plant almost any time during the growing season.**

Container-grown trees and shrubs are grown in pots filled with potting soil and have established root systems. They are most common at garden centres and nurseries. **Container stock is easy to plant, establishes quickly after planting and can be planted almost anytime during the growing season. When choosing a container-grown tree or shrub, make sure it hasn't been in the container too long.** If the roots densely encircle the inside of the pot, then the plant has become rootbound. A rootbound tree or shrub will not establish well, and as the roots mature and thicken, they can choke and kill the plant.

Sometimes, field-grown trees and shrubs are dug and placed in containers instead of burlap; ask if you aren't sure. **Such plants must be treated like balled-and-burlapped stock when planting.**

Bigger is not always better when it comes to choosing woody plants. Smaller plants of a given species often grow up healthier and more robust than larger stock,

particularly in the case of field-grown (as opposed to container-grown) plants. When a plant is dug up out of the field, the roots are severely cut back. The smaller the plant, the more quickly it can recover from the shock of being uprooted.

Improper handling can damage woody plants. You can lift bare-root stock by the stem, but do not lift any other trees or shrubs by the trunk or branches. Rather, lift by the root ball or container, or, if the plant is too large to lift, place it on a tarp or mat and drag it.

Selecting Perennials

Perennials can be purchased as plants or seeds. Purchased plants may begin flowering the same year they are planted, while plants started from seed may take two to three years to mature.

Garden centres, mail-order catalogues and even friends and neighbours are excellent sources of perennials. A number of garden societies promote the exchange of plants and seeds, and many public gardens sell seeds of rare plants. Gardening clubs are also a great source of rare and unusual plants.

Purchased perennials come in two main forms: bare-root and container-grown.

Bare-root perennials consist of pieces of root packed in moist peat moss or sawdust. These roots are typically dormant, although some of the previous year's growth may be evident, or there may be new growth starting. Sometimes the roots appear to have no evident growth, past or present. Bare-root plants are most commonly sold through mail order, but some are available in garden centres, usually in spring. **If you're buying at a garden centre, look for roots that are not overly wilted. There should be no physical damage, and they should be free of insects and diseases. The roots should**

also be dormant (without top growth). A bare-root plant that has been trying to grow in the stressful conditions of a plastic bag may have too little energy to recover or may take longer to establish once planted.

Container-grown perennials come in many sizes. Although a larger plant may appear more mature, a smaller one will suffer less from the shock of being transplanted. **Most perennials grow quickly once they are planted in the garden, so the better buy may well be the smaller plant.**

Select perennials that seem to be a good size for the container they are in. When a plant is tapped lightly out of the container, the roots should be visible but not winding and twisting around the inside of the pot. Healthy roots will appear almost white. Avoid potted plants with very dark, spongy roots that pull away with little effort.

Choose perennials with healthy foliage. If plants appear to be chewed or damaged, check carefully for diseases or insects. Do not purchase a diseased plant. If you find insects on the plant, don't purchase it unless you are willing to cope with the hitchhikers you are taking home.

Selecting Annuals

Annuals can be purchased as plants or seeds. Purchasing transplants is usually easier than starting from seed and provides you with plants that are well grown and often already in bloom. Starting seeds requires space, facilities and time, but offers you a greater selection of plants.

Purchased annuals are grown in a variety of containers. Some are sold in individual containers, some in divided cell-packs and others in undivided trays. Each type has its advantages and disadvantages.

Annuals in individual containers are usually well established and have plenty of space for root growth. The cost of labour, pots and soil can make this option somewhat expensive. If you are planting a large area, you may also find it difficult to transport large numbers of plants this size.

Annuals grown in cell-packs are often inexpensive and hold four to eight plants, making them easy to transport. These annuals suffer less root damage when transplanted than do annuals in undivided trays, but because each cell is quite small, plants may become rootbound quickly.

Annuals grown in undivided trays are inexpensive, they have plenty of room for root growth and they can be left in the trays longer than can plants in other types of containers. Their roots, however, tend to become entangled, making the plants difficult to separate.

Choose plants that are not yet flowering. These plants are younger and are less likely to be rootbound. Plants covered with abundant flowers, with plenty more flower buds on the way, have already passed through a significant portion of their rooting stage, and although they will add instant colour when planted, they will not perform at their best in the heat of summer.

If you buy annuals already in bloom, pinch off the blooms and buds just prior to planting. This encourages new root growth and a bigger show of flowers throughout the season.

Check for roots emerging from the holes at the bottom of the cells, or gently remove the plant from the container to look at the roots. An overabundance of roots means that the plant is too mature for the container, especially if the roots are wrapped around the inside of the container in a thick web. Such plants are slow to establish once they are transplanted into the garden.

Plants should be compact and have good colour. Healthy leaves look firm and vibrant. Unhealthy leaves may be discoloured, chewed or wilted. Tall, leggy plants have likely been deprived of light. Sickly plants may not survive being transplanted and may spread pests or diseases to your garden.

Selecting Bulbs

Bulbs, corms, tubers and rhizomes are modified underground stems, and the selection criteria for each type is very similar. **The following tips, even though they refer only to bulbs, apply to all the different types of underground stems.**

Check the condition of each bulb. Bulbs should be plump, solid and heavy for their size, with no cracks, cuts, scars, mould, soft or squishy spots or blemishes. Note that some bulbs are naturally withered-looking in their healthy state. Avoid bulbs with soft necks or bulbs that have already sprouted.

Select the largest bulbs possible for each variety you intend to grow. In the case of bulbs, big is definitely better. The larger the bulb is, the larger the flowers will be.

Bedding-size bulbs are bulbs with two or three "noses," which are areas on the bulbs where the top growth arises. **These bulbs produce a lot of foliage and flowers and are good for garden and container displays.**

Plant your bulbs as soon as possible after you get them home. Bulbs can be stored in your refrigerator in a paper bag, away from fruits and veggies to minimize ethylene gas exposure, or they can be stored in a cool, dark, dry area until you're ready to plant.

Caring for Purchased Plants

Take care when transporting your new plants from the nursery to your home. Even a short trip can be traumatic for a plant. The heat produced inside a car can quickly dehydrate a plant. If you are using an open vehicle for transport, lay the plants down or cover them to shield them from the wind. Try to avoid mechanical damage such as rubbing or breaking branches and stems during transport.

Purchased plants will need some care until they are planted. **Water the plants if they are dry and keep them in a sheltered, lightly shaded location until planting.** Annuals growing in trays or small containers may require water more than once a day. Remove damaged growth and broken branches from trees and shrubs, but do no other pruning. Get your plants into the ground (or a container) as soon as possible.

Plants purchased in containers can be stored over winter if they can't be planted immediately. Bury the entire container, but not the entire plant, before the ground freezes in fall.

Starting Plants from Seed

One of the most magical parts of gardening is starting plants from seed. To see a tiny, seemingly inert speck germinate and grow to a mature plant over the course of months or years is one of the most gratifying experiences in gardening.

You can grow a much greater variety of plants or cultivars from seed than you could if you relied solely on purchasing bedding plants, but there are some limitations to propagating plants from seed. Some cultivars and varieties don't pass on their desirable traits to their

offspring. Other seeds can take a very long time to germinate, if they germinate at all, and an even longer
time to grow to flowering size.

**It can be very economical to start your plants from
seed if you want or need large numbers of plants.** For
gardeners with large areas to plant, seeds are definitely
a money-saver. The cost of a packet of tomato seeds is
much less than the cost of a six-pack in May; however,
you will need to supply the time and energy to grow
them out from seed instead of having the convenience
of simply purchasing them ready to go.

If you are growing very much from seed, you will
quickly notice that there is a huge variety of seeds.
Some are extremely small, and others are very large.
**Each seed will of course need a different planting
method.**

Purchasing Seeds

**Seeds can be purchased almost everywhere, but the
selection of seeds is often best from mail-order catalogues.** Some seed houses will deal only in specific
types of seeds, while others will carry a good selection
of both flower and vegetable seeds. Seed houses will
carry a large selection of cultivars for gardeners who
desire more choice than a garden centre provides.

As you know, it is difficult to decide what exactly to
plant. When the seed catalogues come, it is usually the
dead of winter and we are dreaming of spring. It is easy
to order more seeds than you have room to plant. **Try
to limit your purchases to what you really want to grow.**
Your local garden centres also have to make these
same kind of choices. They would prefer to have a supply of everything every customer desires, but it is, of
course, impossible to do. Instead, they make the choices
based on what they think most customers will want to
purchase.

Order early to avoid the disappointment of selections being sold out or delays in the delivery of your seed shipment. Choose and order seeds for early starting in spring.

Order gardening and seed catalogues to look through even if you don't start your own seeds. They are welcome when winter is at its height with cold weather and short days that make you yearn for spring.

Collecting Seeds

Many gardeners enjoy the hobby of collecting and planting seeds. **Collecting your own seeds will allow you to maintain varieties of plants that may no longer be sold via commercial means.** Some of these "heirloom" varieties are not readily available, and by saving the seed and growing these plants, you are helping to retain genetic diversity.

You need to know a few basic things before you begin. **Know your plant.** Correctly identify the plant and learn about its life cycle. You will need to know when it flowers, when the seeds are likely to ripen and how the plant disperses its seeds in order to collect them. Research each plant to see if there is a pre-treatment needed to allow for germination. For example, do the seeds need a hot or cold period to germinate?

The easiest way to begin as a seed collector is to collect the seeds from the annual plants in your own garden. Choose plants that are not hybrids, or the seeds will probably not come true to type and may not germinate at all. A few easy plants to collect from are borage, calendula and coriander or cilantro.

When collecting seed, consider the following:

- identify plants that you want to save the seed from by gently tying a soft ribbon around the plant stems when the plant is in full bloom.

• collect seed only from healthy, self-pollinated, non-hybrid plants.

• collect seeds once they are ripe but before they are shed from the parent plant.

• place a paper bag over a seed head as it matures and loosely tie it in place to collect seeds as they are shed.

• finish collecting seeds in late fall or early winter, or when ripe or ready from open-pollinated flowers and vegetables.

• dry seeds after they've been collected. Place them on a paper-lined tray and leave them in a warm, dry location for one to three weeks. Seed from pulpy fruits should be separated, washed and fully dried.

• remove capsules, heads or pods as they begin to dry and remove the seeds later, once they are completely dry.

• store seeds in clearly labeled, air-tight containers in a dry, cool, frost-free location.

Don't collect seeds from the wild. Wild harvesting is severely depleting many plant populations. Some plants you might wish to collect seeds from are rare or endangered in their natural habitats. Many species and populations of wild plants are protected, and it is illegal to collect their seeds.

Treating Seeds

It may be useful to know the anatomy of a seed. A seed is made up of an outer protective layer called the seed coat. The seed coat protects the seed while it is dormant. Beneath the seed coat is the endosperm. The endosperm is the food supply that is essential for the early growth of the seedling. In the centre of the seed is the embryo, which is the minute, undeveloped plant.

103

Some seeds need special conditions in order to germinate. As a general rule, seeds need water, oxygen, the right temperature and sometimes light. Water penetrates the seed coat and causes the endosperm to swell. Nutrients in the endosperm then become available to the embryo so growth can begin. Oxygen is a requirement because the seed must respire in order to break down the food from the endosperm, which provides the energy for the first growth. Every seed has an optimum germination temperature. Above or below the optimum temperature, less seeds will germinate. Light may or may not be needed for germination. Some seeds will be stimulated by light, but others will be inhibited by it at the time of germination. Seeds that need light for germination need to be planted very shallowly. **If you provide optimum conditions for germination, you will in return get the highest germination rate possible for the seeds you are growing.**

Some seeds have built-in protection devices, such as a thick seed coat or poisonous chemicals in the seed coat to deter insects, that prevent them from germinating when conditions are not favourable, or from all germinating at once. In the wild, staggered germination periods improve the chances of survival.

Seeds can be tricked into thinking the conditions are right for sprouting. **Some thick-coated seeds can be soaked for a day or two in a glass of water to promote germination.** This mimics the end of the dry season and the beginning of the rainy season, which is when the plant would germinate in its natural environment. The water softens the seed coat and in some cases washes away the chemicals that have been preventing germination.

Other thick-coated seeds need to be scratched to allow moisture to penetrate the seed coat and prompt germination. This process is called scarification. In nature, birds scratch the seeds with gravel in their craws and acid in their stomachs. Imitate the process by doing one of the following: place the seeds in a bit of sand and move them around; nick the seeds with a knife; gently rub the seeds between two sheets of sandpaper; or tap extremely difficult seeds with a hammer to crack the seed coat. Leave the seeds in a dry place for a day or so after scratching them before planting them. This gives the seeds a chance to get ready for germination before they are exposed to water. Seeds that you might be growing that will need scarification include anemone, clematis, iris and saxifrage.

Plants from northern climates often have seeds that wait until spring before they germinate. **These seeds must be given a cold treatment—called stratification— that mimics winter before they will germinate.** Plant the seeds in a pot or tray and place them in the refrigerator for up to two months. Don't allow the soil to dry out. A less space-consuming method for cold-treating seeds is to mix the seeds with some moistened sand, peat or sphagnum moss. Place the mix in a sealable sandwich bag and pop it in the refrigerator for up to two months, again being sure the sand or moss doesn't dry out.

Starting Seeds

If you have leftover seeds from previous years, sort through them and test them for viability. Simply place a few seeds on a piece of moist paper towel. Keep it moist, and within a short period of time (dependent on the seed type), you should see some sprouting. If you are testing 10 seeds and only five germinate, then you know that your germination rate is 50%, which means you will have to plant twice as many seeds to produce the desired amount of seedlings. Throw out any that don't germinate or that you won't grow.

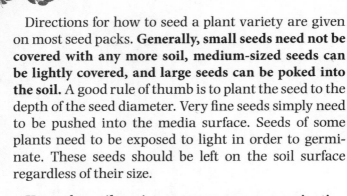

Directions for how to seed a plant variety are given on most seed packs. **Generally, small seeds need not be covered with any more soil, medium-sized seeds can be lightly covered, and large seeds can be poked into the soil.** A good rule of thumb is to plant the seed to the depth of the seed diameter. Very fine seeds simply need to be pushed into the media surface. Seeds of some plants need to be exposed to light in order to germinate. These seeds should be left on the soil surface regardless of their size.

Keep the soil moist to ensure even germination whether you are seeding indoors or directly into the garden. Use a gentle spray to avoid washing the seeds around, or they may pool into dense clumps.

Starting Seeds Indoors

In many areas, the growing season is not long enough for much of what we would like to grow to mature before a killing frost. **Therefore, it is often best for northern gardeners to start seeds indoors under artificial light.** It can be as simple as using inexpensive shop lights with standard fluorescent tubes or as deluxe as purchasing a complete seed-starting growing system that includes adjustable fluorescent grow lights and growing platforms. Ensure that the light you use can be raised and lowered to accommodate the growing plants.

Start seeds easily in cell-packs in trays with plastic dome covers. The cell-packs keep roots separated, and the tray and dome keep moisture in.

Or, start seeds in peat pots or peat pellets. The advantage to starting in peat pots or pellets is that you won't disturb the roots when transplanting the plants into the garden.

When starting seeds indoors, use a planting mix that is intended for seedlings. These mixes are very fine, have good water-holding capacity and will have been sterilized to prevent pests and diseases from attacking your tender young seedlings. One recommended mix for starting seeds is one part peat with one part vermiculite; another is two parts loam with one part peat and one part sharp sand or vermiculite.

Most often, the planting medium is soil-less. **If you are planning to use soil for starting your seeds, take a few precautions.** Soil is a wonderful vector for diseases that attack young seedlings and should be sterilized. You can sterilize soil at home in your microwave or conventional oven.

If you are using a conventional oven, place the soil in a shallow pan; do not pile it more than 10 cm (4") deep. Heat the oven to 82° C (180° F) and "bake" the soil for about 30 minutes. A temperature of 65° C (150° F) will kill off most harmful bacteria and fungi; 70° C (160° F) will kill most insects and viruses; and 80° C (175° F) will take care of most weed seeds. Be advised that soil in the oven will emit an odour that you may not like.

Sterilizing soil in the microwave is a bit faster. One method is to fill clean, litre- (quart-) size containers with moist soil. Cover them with plastic lids that have some holes poked in them to allow the steam to escape, and microwave one container at a time for 90 seconds per kilogram (2.2 pounds) on full power. Leave the soil in the microwave with the door closed for about 20 minutes to complete the process. The temperature inside the microwave needs to be about 95° C (200° F) for those 20 minutes before the soil will be sterilized. As an alternative, place 1 kg (2.2 lb) of moist soil in a plastic bag. Leave the top open and place it in the centre of the microwave. Cook it on high for about 2.5 minutes in a 650-watt microwave. Let the soil cool before planting your seeds.

Moisten seed-starting soil prior to filling your seeding flats or pots, and firm it down in the containers, but don't pack it too tightly. Soil that is too firmly packed will not drain well. Wetting the soil before planting your seeds helps keep the seeds where you plant them.

Plant only one type of seed in each container. Some types of seeds will germinate before others, and it is difficult to keep both seeds and seedlings happy in the same container. Plant one or two large seeds to a cell, but smaller seeds may have to be placed in a folded piece of paper and sprinkled evenly over the soil surface. Very tiny seeds can be mixed with fine sand before being sprinkled evenly across the soil surface.

Seeds can be germinated in a warm spot, such as on top of the refrigerator, or placed on a sunny windowsill. Seeds do not need bright, direct light to germinate and can be kept in an out-of-the-way place until they begin to sprout. However, once germinated, the sun's intensity is not high enough to produce healthy seedlings. Left on the windowsill, the seedlings will become thin and leggy and will not perform well when transplanted into the garden.

Seeds germinate best when the soil remains moist and there is humidity in the air. Place pots or flats of seeds in clear plastic bags to retain humidity while the seeds are germinating. Many planting trays come with clear plastic covers, which can be placed over the trays to keep the moisture in. Change the bag or turn it inside-out once the condensation starts to build up and drip. Plastic bags can be held up with stakes or wires poked in around the edges of the pot. Remove the plastic cover once the seeds have germinated.

Any time the soil or seeds appear dry, spray them with water from a hand-held mister.

For seeds that require heat to germinate, lowering the grow lights to 2.5–5 cm (1–2") above the plastic lid will raise the temperature inside to around 24° C (75° F). Remove the plastic once the seeds have germinated.

Starting Seeds Outdoors

Plants with large or quick-germinating seeds or that are difficult to transplant can be sown directly in the garden. Seeds sown directly into the garden may take longer to germinate than those planted indoors, but the resulting plants will be stronger.

Start with a well-prepared bed that has been smoothly raked. The small furrows left by the rake will help hold moisture and prevent the seeds from being washed away. Then plant seeds according to their size.

- Sprinkle medium-sized seeds onto the soil and cover them lightly with peat moss or more soil.

- Larger seeds can be planted slightly deeper into the soil.

- Place small seeds in the crease of a folded piece of paper and gently tap the bottom of the fold to roll them onto the soil.

- Mix tiny seeds, such as those of begonias, with very fine sand before planting to spread them out more evenly. You may not want to sow very tiny seeds directly in the garden because they can blow or wash away.

When seeding directly into your garden, you can aid germination and protect the seeds by covering your newly seeded bed with chicken wire, an old sheet, some thorny branches or a grow-cover. A cover will discourage pets from digging in the garden. Remove the cover once the seeds have germinated.

Caring for Seedlings

Once seedlings have emerged above the soil, some gardeners set up a small fan to blow over the plants. The air circulation reduces the incidence of some fungal diseases and helps the little seedlings grow strong as they bend and sway in the breeze. Be aware that having a fan will dry out the soil a little quicker, which may mean more frequent watering.

The amount and timing of watering is critical to successfully growing annuals from seed. Most germinated seeds and young seedlings will perish if the soil is allowed to dry out. Strive to maintain a consistently moist soil, which may mean watering lightly every day. As the seedlings get bigger, you can cut back on the amount of times you have to water, but you will have to water a little more heavily. Generally, when the seedlings have their first true leaves (those that look like the adult leaves), you can cut back to watering only when the top 0.25 cm (⅛") of soil has dried.

Small seedlings will not need to be fertilized until they have about four or five true leaves. Seeds provide all the energy and nutrients that younger seedlings require. Fertilizer too early will cause the plants to develop soft growth that is more susceptible to insects and diseases, and too strong a fertilizer can burn tender young roots. When the first leaves that sprouted (seed leaves) begin to shrivel, the plant has used up all its seed energy, so you can begin to apply a fertilizer diluted to quarter-strength.

Seedlings will be weak and floppy if they don't get enough light. It is not possible to grow healthy seedlings indoors without supplemental lighting. **Use a fluorescent or other grow light to provide extra illumination.** If you are using regular fluorescent fixtures, use one warm fluorescent bulb to three cool fluorescent bulbs to ensure that the seedlings get the full light spectrum needed for growth. Place the light 10–13 cm (4–5") above the seedlings and raise it as the seedlings grow to provide enough light intensity for good growth. Check the progress of your seedlings daily.

Damping off is a disease of young seedlings that is caused by a variety of soil-borne fungi. It can devastate young seedlings; one day they're fine, and the next day they seem to have magically disappeared. The fungus is in the medium and causes rapid rotting of the very small seedling stem, so the stem falls over at the surface of the soil. **To prevent seedlings from damping off, always use a sterile soil mix, thoroughly clean containers before using them, maintain good air circulation around seedlings and water from the bottom, keeping the soil moist, not soggy.** It is even better to start your seeds in a soil-less media, which will ensure that there is little chance of damping off occurring. Once seedlings emerge, moisten the soil with a hand-held spray mister when the soil begins to dry out.

Transplanting Seedlings

Transplant seedlings to individual containers once the third true leaf has appeared. Transplanting before this point will be too hard on the young seedlings. Waiting any longer will result in more damage to the seedlings.

The process of transplanting will stimulate feeder roots and of course give plants additional room to grow. Space seedlings so that the leaves do not overshadow those of neighbouring plants. If the seedlings get too big for their containers before you are ready to plant them in your garden, you may have to transplant them to larger pots to prevent them from becoming rootbound. Plants in plug trays can be left until neighbouring leaves start to touch each other. At that point, the plants will be competing for light and should be transplanted to individual pots.

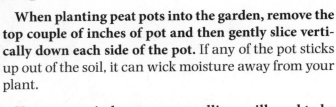

When planting peat pots into the garden, remove the top couple of inches of pot and then gently slice vertically down each side of the pot. If any of the pot sticks up out of the soil, it can wick moisture away from your plant.

Your young, indoor-grown seedlings will need to be hardened off before they get planted into the garden. The process of hardening off is the preparation for seedlings to begin "real life." Start by slowing down the growth of plants by watering less often and reducing the temperature. Then expose them to sunnier, windier conditions and fluctuating outdoor temperatures for increasing periods of time every day for at least a week. Avoid direct sunlight for the first two days.

A cold frame is a mini-greenhouse structure built so that ground level on the inside of the cold frame is lower than on the outside. An angled, hinged lid is fitted with glass. The soil around the outside of the cold frame insulates the plants inside. The lid lets light in and collects some heat during the day and prevents rain from damaging tender plants. If the interior gets too hot, the lid can be raised for ventilation. A cold frame is a wonderful tool because it takes a lot of the work out of the hardening off process.

If you don't have a cold frame, wait until all danger of frost has passed before transplanting seedlings. A cool, cloudy, still day is ideal for transplanting, but at the very least, do not transplant in the heat of the day. Water in your transplants with a dilute concentration of high-phosphorus fertilizer.

Seeding Vegetables

Every type of seed has a period of viability that is useful as a guide to how long seeds can be stored. Corn, onion and parsnip seeds will last only one year under optimum conditions. Okra, parsley and salsify seeds will generally last about two years in storage. If you have any of these seeds from more than two years ago, throw them out. Beet, broccoli, Brussels sprout, cabbage, cauliflower, celery, cucumber, eggplant, endive, kale, lettuce, muskmelon, radish, rutabaga, spinach, squash and turnip seeds will last up to five years under optimum conditions.

Vegetables are relatively easy to germinate; most of them need nothing more than moisture and temperatures around 21–32° C (70–90° F). Warming up vegetable beds with row covers allows many plants and seeds to be sown early, especially warm-season plants such as beans or sweet corn. Cool-season plants such as peas, carrots and parsnips can be sown into cool soil with no detrimental effects.

Sow the following vegetable seeds directly into the garden: beans (both bush and pole), beets, carrots, collards, corn, cucumbers, endive, kale, kohlrabi, mustard greens, parsnips, peas, potatoes, radishes, spinach, squash (both summer and winter), swiss chard and turnips.

Start the following vegetables indoors:

• Brussels sprouts and lettuce 4–6 weeks before last spring frost

• basil, broccoli, cabbage, cauliflower, celeriac, celery and tomatoes 6–8 weeks before last spring frost

• chives, eggplant, leeks, parsley and marjoram 8–10 weeks before last spring frost

• onions 10–12 weeks before last spring frost.

Vegetable gardens may need a push during seasons experiencing drought. Plant early when conditions allow. Short-season vegetable varieties such as onions, potatoes, garlic, lettuce, peas and spinach are ideal

during a drought because they're in and out of the ground faster than other vegetables, resulting in less water use.

Use your space wisely. Plant vegetables close together in wide beds. High-density plantings minimize the amount of space needed for paths between the rows. Interplant species that have similar needs but different lengths of time until maturity. For example, try planting lettuce or other fresh greens close to carrots. The lettuce will finish first, leaving the carrots the space they need to complete their growth.

Growing vegetables in containers can be good. Use some of the shorter cultivars to ensure the container provides enough soil for optimum growth. Bush beans, small beets, mini carrots, bush cucumbers, leaf lettuce, herbs, peppers and tomatoes are only a few of the vegetables that can be grown successfully in containers.

Planting

If you've planned your garden, prepared your soil and selected your plants, it's time for the fun part: planting. So go ahead and dig in.

General Planting Tips

Pre-Planting

The most important factor in ensuring the survival of a plant in your garden is where you plant it. Find out what the best growing conditions are for your new plant to thrive, and then plant it where those conditions exist in your yard. A shrub that needs full sun will never do well in a north-facing location.

Group plants together that have similar needs. Learn all about the plants you are including in your landscape so that plants with the same environmental needs, such as water-loving plants, shade-tolerant plants or drought-resistant plants, can be grouped to simplify maintenance and to help prevent problems with pests and diseases.

Before you pick up a shovel and start digging, be certain to have all utility locations identified and marked off. Many provinces have a "One Call" or "1st Call" service that will prompt all utility companies to mark the gas, electric, phone and any other underground utility lines. Your local government offices will usually have the phone number handy if you can't find it.

Invest in a selection of good garden tools. They can be expensive. Start with a few basics—a good quality

garden fork, flat-bladed shovel, trowel, hand-pruners and rake—and gradually add specialized tools. Purchase the best quality tools you can afford. Good quality tools will last longer and do a better job.

If you have started any plants indoors, remember that the light intensity inside the home—even in a south-facing window—is much less than it would be outside that pane of glass. **Begin to harden off the plants by placing them outdoors for a short period each day.** It sometimes seems like a lot of work to move the plants in and out, but doing so gives your plants time to adapt to outdoor weather conditions and reduces the chance of transplant shock.

Get your purchased plants into the ground as soon as possible when you get them home. Roots can get hot and dry out quickly in containers. Keep plants in a shady spot if you must wait to plant them. However, to avoid added stress to those tender seedlings, remember to harden them off into the conditions in which they will be growing by gradually exposing them to longer periods of time in the sun. Not acclimatizing your plant can damage and burn the foliage and will set the plant back from its normal growth cycle.

Planting

Remove containers before planting. Plastic and fibre pots restrict root growth and prevent plants from becoming established.

Be careful not to disturb the root tissue any more than necessary. However, if the plant has been in the container too long, the roots will be growing in an unnatural fashion and will have to be encouraged to grow out of the current root ball.

Most plants are happiest when planted at the same depth at which they have always grown. Trees, in particular, can be killed by too deep a planting. There are some exceptions to this rule, but make sure you know which plants can withstand a change in depth. Tomatoes are one plant that comes to mind that can be planted quite a bit deeper, which is a wonderful solution to tall, leggy tomato plants.

When planting annuals and perennials into a prepared bed that you intend to mulch, you have two choices. **Plant all the plants and then mulch around them, or save some time and mulch the bed first, and then plant through the mulch.**

When planting into containers for a container garden, the planting medium used is extremely important. You want something that is lightweight and uniform and that will hold moisture but is still well drained. **Two parts peat moss to one part perlite and one part vermiculite, with some slow-release fertilizer, is a winning combination for any container.** If you prefer to use soil, use two parts soil and two parts peat moss to one part vermiculite and one part perlite.

In a cool year, wait until after the risk of frost has passed completely to give the soil more time to warm up before planting tender, heat-loving plants. Cool, wet spring weather can cause some drought-loving plants to rot.

Avoid planting during the hottest, sunniest part of the day. Choose an overcast day, or plant early or late in the day. The transplants will be less stressed and will have a better chance to become established than if you planted them on a hot, dry day.

Many plants, especially those that are container-grown, can be planted at any time of year as long as they can be properly maintained. **Avoid planting during the hottest and driest part of summer, when plants suffer the immediate effects of transplant shock combined with the stress of blistering sun and heat.**

After you have transplanted your bedding plants, water them in with a "starter" solution. You can either purchase a starter solution from your favourite garden centre, or you can simply use a high-phosphorus fertilizer that has been diluted down. This small chore will help reduce the stress of transplanting and will help your transplants root in as quickly as possible.

Post-Planting

Often, just when we've got our tender plants in the ground, there is a forecast of impending frost overnight. **To protect plants from a sudden blast of freezing weather, cover them with cloth.** Don't use plastic because it has no insulating value.

Always treat your tools with respect. **After using a tool, wash off any soil or debris that might be clinging to the tool before putting it away.** Tools that are put away clean will stay sharper and make the work for the operator easier. Regular sharpening, cleaning and oiling of your tools will ensure they serve you for a long time.

Planting Trees and Shrubs

A tree or shrub that is planted correctly will be more tolerant of the normal stresses that will be encountered. The quality of planting will always have an influence on how water (and therefore nutrients) move within the soil, thus influencing the uptake by the tree. Try to emulate the conditions where the tree or shrub was grown previously.

Where to Plant

Before you worry about how to plant, you need to consider where to plant. **Don't plant trees or shrubs within 1 m (40") of underground electric or gas lines.** Even if you don't damage anything by digging, the roots may cause trouble in the future, or the plant may have to be cut down if the pipes or wires ever need servicing.

Know the mature size of any plant you intend to put into your landscape, especially if it is a tree or shrub. The plant you have purchased or acquired is immature and likely pretty small. When planting anything new, always think about the mature size. Is it far enough away from the house, driveway and walkways? Will it hit the overhang of the house or any overhead power lines? Once it reaches its mature height and spread, will it still fit the space you have chosen? If you have not planned for the mature size of the tree or shrub, there will be problems in the future. Crowded trees and shrubs will never grow to their potential. Worse yet, during their growth, they will be more susceptible to insect and disease problems due to the stress of overcrowding. It is always difficult to make the decision to remove a problem tree in the landscape, but if it has been planted in the wrong place or without adequate room to grow, then removing it is often the only real solution.

If you're planting several shrubs, make sure that they won't be growing too close together once they are fully grown. **Normally, to determine the spacing, add the mature spreads and then divide by two.** For example, when planting a shrub with an expected spread of 1.2 m (4') next to one with an expected spread of 1.8 m (6'), you would plant them 1.5 m (5') apart.

The rule is slightly different if you are trying to create a windbreak. With hedges, you want to ensure that there are no spaces. **To avoid gaps in hedges and windbreaks when they reach maturity, space the plants at one-half to two-thirds of their mature spread.** They will grow to create a semi-solid barrier from the wind. It can be difficult to decide how far apart to place the plants in your hedge, but resist planting them too close

to each other; any hedge will gradually increase in size, despite shearing, so allow room for this expansion when planting.

When to Plant

The next consideration is when to plant. **For most trees, planting in early spring is best.** That way the trees will have the whole growing season to establish themselves before winter sets in. The second-best time to plant trees is late summer. You avoid the intense summer heat, and the plants have a couple of months to establish root systems before slipping into winter dormancy.

Container-grown stock can essentially be planted any time in the year. Try to transplant balled-and-burlapped stock when the tree or shrub is not in active growth and the transpiration needs are lowest—plant in early spring if possible.

How to Plant

Finally, you will need to consider how to plant. **Trees and shrubs should always be planted at the depth at which they were growing, or just above the roots if you are unsure of the depth for bare-root stock.** Be sure that the plant is not set too deeply. Planting even 5–10 cm (2–4") too deep can cause problems. Planting too shallow exposes the root ball to the drying effects of sun and wind and will likely result in transplant failure.

When digging the planting hole for balled-and-burlapped or container-grown trees or shrubs, the depth in the centre of the hole should equal the depth of the root ball. It is usually helpful to dig deeper around the centre ledge. This hole shape prevents the plant from sinking as the soil settles and encourages excess water to drain away from the new plant. The width of the hole should be at least twice the width of the root ball.

Rough up the sides and bottom of a tree or shrub planting hole to aid in root transition and water flow. It is also good practice to loosen the soil for a distance beyond the hole with a garden fork.

If planting into a heavy soil, raise the plant about 2.5 cm (1") above the soil surface to help improve surface drainage away from the crown and roots.

When planting grafted stock, keep the graft union above ground to make it easy to spot and remove suckers sprouting from the rootstock. However, some plants, such as grafted roses, are planted with the graft union below the soil surface.

Mix a few handfuls to a shovelful of compost into the backfill soil. This small amount will encourage the plant to become established, but too much creates a pocket of rich soil that the roots may be reluctant to move beyond. If the roots do not venture beyond the immediate area of the hole, the tree or shrub will be weaker and much more susceptible to problems, and the encircling roots could eventually choke the plant. Such a tree will also be more vulnerable to being blown over in a strong wind.

Backfill to the same depth at which the plant was grown previously for container stock, or just above the root ball or root mass for balled-and-burlapped or bare-root stock. Avoid piling backfill soil around the stem or stems.

When backfilling your trees and shrubs, it is important to have good root-to-soil contact for initial stability and good establishment. If large air pockets remain after backfilling, the result could be excessive settling and root drying. **Use water to settle backfill soil gently around the roots and in the hole, being careful not to drown the plant.** Fill in small amounts rather than everything all at once. Add some soil, then water it

down, repeating until the hole is full. Stockpile any soil that remains after backfilling and use it to top up the soil around the plant as the backfill settles.

If you are working with a heavy clay soil, ensure that the surface drainage slopes away from your new transplant.

☙ Container-Grown Stock

Before planting a containerized tree or shrub, check to make sure you know the depth of the root ball. Most potted, field-grown trees are planted deeply in the pot to keep the freshly dug tree from tipping over, and there may be mulch on top of the soil as well. Scrape off the mulch or soil until you find the root mass and then plant just above it.

The soil in the container is not likely to be the same as the soil you just removed from the planting hole. **The extra size of the hole allows the new roots an easier place to grow into than undisturbed soil, providing an easy transition zone from the root ball soil to the existing on-site soil.**

Containers for container stock are usually made of plastic or pressed fibre. **Both kinds should be removed before planting.** Although some containers appear to be made of peat moss, they do not decompose well. The roots may have difficulty penetrating the pot sides, and the fibre will wick moisture away from the roots.

Gently remove or cut off the container and look at the root mass to see whether the plant is rootbound. If roots are circling around the inside of the container, they should be loosened or sliced. **Any large roots encircling or growing into the centre of the root mass instead of outward should be removed before planting.** A sharp pair of hand pruners or a pocketknife will work well for this task.

𝔇 Balled-and-Burlapped Stock

The burlap used for balled-and-burlapped stock was originally made out of natural fibres that would eventually decompose. Modern burlap may or may not be made of natural fibres, and it can be difficult to tell the difference. Synthetic fibres will not decompose and will eventually choke the roots. **Remove as much of the burlap as you can from around the root ball to prevent girdling and to maximize contact between the roots and the soil.** If roots are growing through the burlap, try to avoid damage to these new roots while removing it. You may need to cut away the burlap with a knife or scissors.

If your balled-and-burlapped stock comes in a wire basket, remove the basket. You may need strong wire cutters to get the basket off. If the tree is very heavy, it may not be possible to remove the base of the basket, but cut away at least the sides, where most of the important roots will be growing.

𝔇 Bare-Root Stock

The shape of the planting hole for bare-root stock is somewhat different than for balled-and-burlapped or containerized stock. **Make sure the hole is deep and wide enough to allow the roots to fully extend, with some extra width on the sides. The hole should have a central cone to help fan out and support the roots and to keep the plant centred.**

The advantage to planting bare-root stock is economical. Harvesting, storing and transporting bare-root stock is infinitely cheaper because of the lack of soil around the roots. **Before planting bare-root stock, remove the plastic and sawdust from the roots. Trim damaged roots prior to planting. Always plant bare-root trees and shrubs when they are dormant. Soak the entire root system in a bucket of water for 12 hours prior to planting. Large trees must be staked until well-established.**

After You Plant

When planting trees or shrubs, remove only those branches that have been damaged during transport and planting. Do not remove any top growth to make up for roots lost when the plant was dug out of the field unless you have seriously damaged the root tissue. Plants need all the branches and leaves they have when they are trying to get established; the top growth produces the energy and hormones necessary to stimulate root growth. There is a balance between the top and the root growth of every plant. Try to maintain that balance. Allow your new plant to settle in for a year or two before you start any formative pruning.

A treewell, which is a temporary, 5–10 cm (2–4") high, doughnut-like mound of soil around the perimeter of the planting hole to capture extra water, is an excellent tool for conserving water, especially during dry spells. Use this reservoir for at least the first season, and two seasons at most. In periods of heavy rain, you may need to breach the treewell to prevent plant roots from becoming waterlogged. Rebuild the treewell when drier conditions resume.

To conserve water, mulch around new tree and shrub plantings. Composted wood chips or shredded bark will stay where placed. Do not use too much—5–10 cm

(2–4") is adequate—and avoid mulching directly against the trunk or base of the plant, which can encourage disease problems.

Staking Tips

Some trees may need to be staked in order to provide support while the roots establish. Staking is recommended only for bare-root trees, top-heavy trees over 1.5 m (5') tall or trees planted in windy locations (particularly evergreens, which tend to catch winter winds). The stakes should be removed as soon as the roots have had a chance to become established, which normally takes about a year.

Growing trees and shrubs without stakes is preferable because unstaked trees develop more roots and stronger trunks. Most newly planted trees can stand on their own without staking. You can always stake later if you find it's needed.

The two-stake method is suitable for small trees (about 1.5–1.8 m [5–6'] tall) and for trees in low-wind areas:

- Drive two tall, sturdy stakes into the soil on directly opposite sides of the tree, in line with the prevailing wind and just outside the planting hole. Driving the stakes too near the tree can damage the roots and will not provide adequate support.

- Tie strong cord, rope, cable or wire to the stakes. The end that goes around the trunk should be a wide, belt-like strap of material that will not injure the trunk. Your local garden centre should have ties designed for this purpose, or you can cushion the rope or wire with a section of rubber hose.

- Attach the straps to the tree about 1–1.2 m (3–4') above the ground.

Never wrap rope, wire or cable directly around a tree trunk. Always use non-damaging material.

Reposition the strapping every two to three months to prevent any rubbing or girdling injury.

Never tie trees so firmly that they can't move. Young trees need to be able to move in the wind to produce strong trunks and to develop roots more thickly in appropriate places to compensate for the prevailing wind.

Don't leave the stakes in place too long. One year is sufficient for almost all trees. The stakes should be there only long enough to give the roots some time to grow and establish. The tree will actually be weaker if the stakes are left for too long, and over time the ties can damage the trunk and weaken or kill the tree.

Transplanting Tips

Transplant trees and shrubs only when it is necessary. With planning and forethought, you should not need to transplant any tree or shrub after its initial placement.

If you must move a tree or shrub, timing is important. Evergreens can be transplanted in spring before growth starts, or later in the season after it stops, as long as it is not during a spell of hot weather. Deciduous plants should be transplanted only while dormant—when the branches are bare of leaves in early spring, late fall or early winter.

The younger the tree or shrub, the more likely it is to re-establish successfully when moved to a new location. For every 2.5 cm (1") of trunk diameter, it typically takes one year for a tree to become well established after transplanting.

When woody plants are transplanted, they inevitably lose most of their root mass. **Take care to dig a root**

ball of an appropriate size. As a general guideline, for every 2.5 cm (1") of main stem width, which is measured 15–30 cm (6–12") above the ground, you need to excavate a root ball at least 30 cm (12") wide and deep, and preferably larger.

Root balls are heavy. **A 60 cm (24") root ball is probably the most the average gardener can manage without heavy equipment, although you may still require extra assistance.** Trees with trunks more than 5 cm (2") in diameter should be moved by professionals.

The size of root balls for shrubs cannot always be measured as easily as trees, so you will need to use your best judgment. Large shrubs are best moved by professionals. It may be easier to start with a new one rather than try to move a very large specimen.

If it is necessary and feasible to transplant a shrub or small tree, follow these steps:

1) Calculate the size of the root ball to be removed, as described previously.

2) Water the root ball area to a depth of 30 cm (12") and allow excess water to drain away. The moist soil will help hold the root ball together.

3) Wrap or tie the branches to minimize branch damage and to ease transport from the old site to the new one.

4) Slice a long spade or shovel into the soil vertically, cutting a circle the size of the calculated root ball around the plant. Cut down to about 30 cm (12"). This depth should contain most of the roots for the size of tree or shrub that can be transplanted manually.

5) At this point, most small, densely rooted trees and shrubs can be carefully removed from the

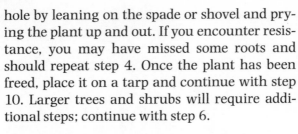

hole by leaning on the spade or shovel and prying the plant up and out. If you encounter resistance, you may have missed some roots and
should repeat step 4. Once the plant has been
freed, place it on a tarp and continue with step
10. Larger trees and shrubs will require additional steps; continue with step 6.

6) Cut another circle one shovel-width outside the
first circle, to the same depth.

7) Excavate the soil between the two cut circles.

8) Carefully cut horizontally under the root ball.
When you encounter a root, cut it with a pair of
hand pruners or loppers. The goal is to sculpt
out a root ball that is standing on a pedestal of
undisturbed earth.

9) Spread a tarp in the hole to the side of the plant.
Gently remove the pedestal and lean the root
ball over onto the tarp. Carefully cut any remaining roots in the pedestal. Lift the plant and root
ball out of the hole using the tarp, not by the
stem or branches.

10) Lift or drag the tarp to the new location and replant the tree or shrub immediately. Transplanted trees and shrubs can be treated as
balled-and-burlapped stock.

The care you give your new tree or shrub in the first
three years after planting or transplanting is the most
important. **During this period of establishment, it is
critical to remove competing weeds, to keep the plant
well watered and to avoid all mechanical damage.** Be
careful with lawn mowers and string trimmers, which
can quickly girdle the base of the plant. Whatever you do
to the top of the plant affects the roots, and vice versa.

Planting Bare-Root Perennials

Cut off any damaged parts of the roots of bare-root perennials with a very sharp knife or garden scissors.

Soak the roots in lukewarm water for one to two hours to rehydrate them. Do not leave them in water longer than that, or you may encourage root or crown rot.

Bare-root perennials will dehydrate quickly out of soil, so they need to be planted more quickly than potted plants. **Plant the roots either directly in the garden or into pots with good-quality potting soil until they can be moved to the garden.**

It may be difficult to distinguish the top from the bottom of some bare-root plants. Usually there is a telltale dip or stub from which the plant previously grew. **If you can't find any distinguishing characteristics, lay the root in the soil on its side, and the plant will send the roots down and the shoots up.**

Planting Bulbs

Spring-flowering bulbs are a wonderful addition to any landscape. **Because they need a period of cold (stratification) to initiate bloom, they must be planted in fall.** So spend those last crisp, sunny fall days digging in the garden preparing for the wonderful blooms of spring. Tulips, daffodils, crocuses, scillas, muscaris and alliums are just a few of the bulbs whose flowers will welcome you back into the garden next year.

When deciding where to plant those bulbs, envision your garden in early spring just when the snow is receding. Continue to imagine what you see throughout April and May until the leaves come out on all of the deciduous trees. What a beautiful sight in spring it is to view tiny little scillas poking their leaves and blooms through the receding snow banks on your front lawn.

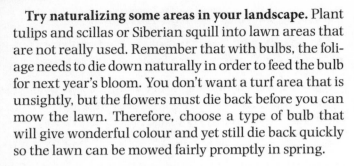

Try naturalizing some areas in your landscape. Plant tulips and scillas or Siberian squill into lawn areas that are not really used. Remember that with bulbs, the foliage needs to die down naturally in order to feed the bulb for next year's bloom. You don't want a turf area that is unsightly, but the flowers must die back before you can mow the lawn. Therefore, choose a type of bulb that will give wonderful colour and yet still die back quickly so the lawn can be mowed fairly promptly in spring.

If you are instead planting bulbs in a normal bed-type planting, try to envision the spring show of blooms. **It is generally a better show if you plant in large masses of colour rather than a small grouping of similar bulbs.** Waves of colour are show-stopping, while a few bulbs here and there are pleasant, but don't come close to the display that could be possible.

A general planting guide is to plant most tulips about 20 cm (8") deep and on average 15 cm (6") apart. Smaller bulbs such as scilla, crocus and grape hyacinth can be planted about 7 cm (3") deep and about the same in spread.

Bulbs like to have sufficient moisture but abhor being soggy. **Plant them in an area where the soil is well drained but rich in organic matter.**

Allow bulblets to naturally separate from the mother bulb, rather than forcing them apart. Bulbs that are in the process of separating often have two or more "noses" and will produce more foliage and flowers than single-nosed bulbs. Daughter bulblets that have been forced apart prematurely may take a couple of years before they bloom.

Planting Out-of-Zone Plants

Before planting, observe your garden on a frosty morning. Do some areas escape frost? They are potential sites for tender plants. Keep in mind that cold air tends to collect in low spots and can run downhill and through breaks in plantings and structures, much like water does.

Provide shelter from the prevailing wind. Plants that are not truly hardy to your zone will suffer from stress more easily than the very hardy plants. Plant in groups to create windbreaks and microclimates. Rhododendrons, for instance, grow better if they are planted in small groups or grouped with plants that have similar growing requirements.

Planting Ornamental Grasses

Many ornamental grasses have great four-season appeal in a landscape. The new growth often emerges in early spring. The clumps of foliage flow and dance with even the gentlest breeze through summer. The flower spikes grow and expand into fall, when the whole plant takes on a golden brown colour that persists through winter.

Plant your ornamental grasses in spring to ensure they have plenty of time to establish prior to winter.

Space your grasses far enough apart to allow for their distinctive form to be fully appreciated. Grasses that are placed too close together will also have limited movement, which means you are giving up some of the aesthetic pleasure they bring.

For the first couple of years after planting, you will need to ensure that they get adequate moisture, but once established, most ornamental grasses are really quite drought tolerant.

Ornamental grasses whose blades arch or flop over are excellent plants for softening the edges of beds, borders and containers. Tall, upright ornamental grasses make a wonderful temporary hedge.

There are basically two types of grasses. **Cool season grasses grow best when temperatures are cool and moisture is plentiful.** Our most typical cool season grass is Kentucky blue grass, which is the main component of our lawns. Cool season grasses will go dormant when the temperature soars if there is not sufficient irrigation. Some other cool season grasses that we grow include the lovely blue fescue and statuesque feather reed grass, both fabulous additions to any landscape.

Warm season grasses are those grasses that thrive under warmer conditions. They are sluggish in spring and find their niche when temperatures are over 24° C (75° F). Most warm season grasses will not survive severe winters, but sometimes, with adequate snow cover and the right microclimate, grasses such as miscanthus 'Morning Light' will make it to spring.

More General Planting Tips

Large trees that cast very dense shade do not allow very much to grow under them. So what can you plant underneath evergreen trees? **Sometimes, at least close to the tree trunk, organic mulch is all that is needed. Placing a few feature rocks is sometimes a nice touch. Many trees will allow hardy groundcovers such as lily-of-the-valley or periwinkle to grow at their feet.** One wonderful choice is bergenia, which does extremely well under evergreen trees in sun or shade, thrives with very little water and looks wonderful year-round.

Turn a windswept area into a sheltered one with a hedge. Hedges and trees temper the wind's effect without the turbulence found on the leeward side of more solid structures such as walls or fences. Any vertical form in the landscape will change how the wind blows. The wind will hit the hedge and some of the air will pass through, but most will move over top of the hedge. How high the hedge or other vertical form is will determine how long it will take the wind to fall back down. Sometimes, you will find that you can tuck a small seating area on the leeward side of the hedge and enjoy almost no wind at all.

Do not plant turfgrass right up to the base of any tree or shrub. Trees and shrubs require different soil conditions than turfgrass, such as a more acidic and more fungally dominated soil. Trees and shrubs compete very well for water and nutrient resources with turfgrass but have very different maintenance requirements. Create a mulched area at least out to the drip line of the tree or shrub. This area reduces the chance of mechanical damage, such as mower injury, to the tree or shrub and helps separate the different maintenance regimes.

If you like flowering trees but don't like the messy fruit that often follows, try growing small-fruited trees such as cherries or saskatoons. Plant them in large flower beds or borders or in another place where the falling fruit won't spoil your lawn or stain your deck, porch or driveway.

Herbs are often overlooked as landscape plants, but their foliage, fragrance, flowers and low-maintenance requirements are a welcome addition to any garden. Grow your herbs organically and use them fresh in your gourmet food preparation. You can plant containers with specific plant and herb combinations for your favourite dishes, such as a salsa container or a pesto container.

Many plants have flowers or foliage with intoxicating aromas. **Plant them where the fragrance can be enjoyed, such as under a window, near a doorway or path or on your patio in a container.**

Plant spring-flowering perennials such as primroses and candytuft for an early blast of colour after a long winter.

When planting up a container, follow the same design principles you would if you were doing a bouquet in a vase. **Keep the chosen plants and the container in scale.** The mature height of the plants should be about 2.5 times the height of the container. Following this guideline will ensure your container looks in proportion.

Put trailing plants near the edge of a container to spill out and bushy and upright plants in the middle where they will give height and depth to the planting. The root zone in a container can heat up in the hot sun. Trailing plants will shade the sides of the container.

Consider mixing different plants together in a container. You can create contrasts of colour, texture and habit and give a small garden an inviting appearance. Different plant textures such as tall and spiky mixed with round and soft make an interesting mix. Fountain grass mixed with wave petunias and a few cosmos is interesting throughout the growing season. Experiment with colours you find attractive. Try opposites such as purples with yellows or softer combinations of pinks and purples.

Don't be afraid to combine annuals, perennials, bulbs, herbs, vines, groundcovers, vegetables, fruits and shrubs together for varied and attractive plantings, as long as the cultural requirements for the plants are similar.

Be aware of how your plants propagate. Many plants reproduce by more than seed and can spread aggressively if not contained. **Plant aggressive plants in containers or in garden beds that have barriers to prevent escape.**

Maintenance

Prevention is the most important aspect of problem management. A healthy garden is resistant to problems and develops a natural balance between beneficial and detrimental organisms. Take the time to maintain your garden so that you can enjoy your garden.

Seasonal Maintenance

Spring

While you are waiting for the weather to warm up enough for you to plant, you can keep busy doing many little chores that will get you outside and busy and at least closer to the garden. Thoroughly clean empty planters, containers and seed trays to get them ready for spring planting. Bring garden tools out of storage and examine them for rust or other damage. Clean, oil and sharpen them if you didn't before you put them away in fall.

Wait for your garden to dry out somewhat before working the soil, or even walking through it, to prevent soil compaction. Never work with your soil in early spring when it's very wet or very dry. In many regions, April is the time that you can first get into the garden and begin to get ready for the growing season.

Once the soil is workable, you can begin the spring cleanup. Rake debris off lawns and prune back old perennial growth. Pull back mulch from sprouting plants on warm days in spring, but be prepared to cover plants back over on cold nights.

Be careful not to encourage too much growth too early; those early shoots are very susceptible to damage. Sometimes, plants that are not placed in the best possible location poke their heads up too early in spring. A common problem is to see some tulips sprouting through the snow very early in spring. This may seem to be a good thing, but growth that is too early will likely result in no growth for the season. Early-spring flowering bulbs are best planted on any exposure other than south to ensure that they come up early, but not so early that they get hit by frost.

Ornamental grasses are relatively carefree, except for the annual cutting back that is necessary each spring. **Cut back your grasses prior to any new growth occurring.** Waiting until late spring will result in many of the tips being cut off, which reduces their attractiveness. Most grasses will need to be cut back to a few centimetres above the soil. Many of the cool season grasses will begin their growth early in spring.

Do not cut back the green foliage of bulb plants such as daffodils and tulips. The foliage is providing energy to the roots and bulbs for next year's growth. The foliage can be cut back when it has turned brown and dried up.

Train new shoots of climbing vines, such as morning glories and sweet peas, to their supports to ensure that wind or passersby do not damage the tender growth. A couple of minutes each day to get them growing in the right direction is much easier than trying to tame large growth later.

Summer

Remove dead flowers from plants. Deadheading encourages more flowering and keeps displays looking tidy. Deadhead repeat-blooming annuals, perennials and roses regularly to keep them looking their best.

Like every other plant grown in the landscape, your vegetables need space to grow to their potential. **Thin vegetable crops such as beets, carrots and turnips early in the season to allow for optimum growth.** Crowded plants lead to poor crops.

Top up the level of water in water gardens regularly during hot and dry spells if levels drop because of evaporation.

Vines grown on a chain-link fence are more exposed to the environment than vines grown against a wall. **Give them extra water to compensate for any extra drying from the wind or sun.**

During the regular growing season, lightly pinch back your late-flowering perennials to help them bush out. Shearing some annuals and perennials back will encourage new growth, giving them a fresh look for fall.

Replace fading flowers and vegetables by sowing seeds for a fall display or crop. Peas, bush beans, annual candytuft and lobelia are often finished fruiting or blooming by mid- to late summer, leaving holes in the garden that can be filled by new plants. Seeds for replacement plants can be directly sown or started indoors.

If you've let your weeds get out of hand over summer, be sure to pull them up before they set seed to avoid having even more weeds popping up in the garden next summer.

Fall
✍ *Protecting Your Plants*
Wrap some protection around your trees. Loosely wrap tree trunks, particularly of young trees, with trunk covers from the garden centre to prevent them from splitting during the

freeze/thaw portion of the year. Gently and loosely wrap chicken wire or wire mesh around the base of tree trunks to prevent animals from chewing off the bark underneath the snow.

Keep an eye open in fall for pests that may be planning to hibernate in the debris around your plants or in the bark of your trees. Taking care of a few insects in fall may keep several generations out of your garden next summer.

Water your plants thoroughly before the ground freezes in winter. This will ensure that the plants have the water necessary for growth early in spring and will also reduce temperature fluctuations during freeze and thaw cycles throughout the winter months.

If you are experimenting with out-of-zone plants, mulch young specimens in fall, at least for their first two years, with a thick layer of clean organic mulch such as bark chips, composted woodchips, composted leaves or compost mixed with peat moss. Good winter protection requires a depth of 15–20 cm (6–8").

Mound mulch around the bases of semi-hardy shrubs to protect the roots and stem bases from temperature fluctuations. Start mulching the garden in fall, but avoid covering plants completely until the ground has frozen. Waiting prevents plants from rotting and deters small rodents from digging down and feasting on plant roots and crowns. Find a source of straw for mulch in early to mid-fall, because it can be harder to find later in the season when you're ready to begin covering up your beds for winter.

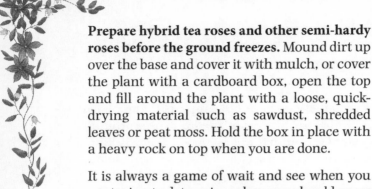

Prepare hybrid tea roses and other semi-hardy roses before the ground freezes. Mound dirt up over the base and cover it with mulch, or cover the plant with a cardboard box, open the top and fill around the plant with a loose, quick-drying material such as sawdust, shredded leaves or peat moss. Hold the box in place with a heavy rock on top when you are done.

It is always a game of wait and see when you are trying to determine when you should cover your tender shrubs. **It is best to wait for the ground to freeze up before covering or wrapping tender shrubs and evergreens to ensure that all growth has slowed for winter.** Use a layer of burlap or horticultural cloth, or use special insulating blankets available at garden centres.

Winterizing Your Garden

Rake up all of the leaves that have fallen from your deciduous plants and clean up any plant debris from your flower beds, including the borders. The leaves can be used in different ways: add them to the compost pile; gather them into their own compost pile to decompose into leaf mould; or mow over them and then pile them onto flower beds—whole leaves can become matted together, encouraging fungal disease.

Unless your plants have been afflicted with some sort of disease, you can leave faded perennial growth in place and clean it up in spring. The stems will collect any missed leaves and snow, protecting the roots and crown of the plant over winter.

Weed the garden and mow the lawn one last time. This is the perfect opportunity to use the mulching attachment or option on your mower.

Spread a thin layer of good quality, screened soil combined with compost over your lawn and rake it in for a good fall feed. This mixture can also be spread over beds without a decorative mulch layer on top.

Fall is a great time to improve your soil. Amendments added now can be worked in lightly. By planting time next spring, the amendments will have been further worked in by the actions of worms and other soil microorganisms and by the freezing and thawing that takes place over winter.

Continue to water the garden in fall during dry spells to prevent the soil from drying out entirely. Consistent watering in fall helps prepare plants for winter. Apply an organic anti-desiccant to newly planted evergreens to reduce winter moisture loss.

Move clay and concrete pots and statues into a protected location to prevent them from cracking over winter. The very low temperatures that are experienced in many of our areas can do a lot of damage to clay pots that are not constructed to withstand extreme cold. Clay pots can be emptied, cleaned and stored indoors for winter.

Clean tools thoroughly and wipe them with an oily rag to prevent them from rusting before storing them for winter.

Winter

Snow is the garden's best friend. **Pile clean snow on snowless garden beds to insulate them against the wind and cold.** Some people refer to this as "snow farming."

Check shrubs and trees throughout the winter months or while they are dormant for storm-damaged branches, and remove them using proper pruning techniques.

Water shrubs and evergreens during winter thaws if there is no snow around them. Water the ground around the plants, but don't worry if some water freezes onto the branches—a little bit of ice won't hurt them.

Gently brush snow off the branches of evergreens such as cedars, but leave any ice that forms to melt naturally. The weight of the snow or ice can permanently bend flexible branches, but more damage is done trying to remove ice than is done through its weight.

Get lawn mowers and other power tools serviced prior to spring. They will be ready for use in spring, and you may get a better price before the big rush.

Pruning

Pruning is essential to the health of your woody ornamentals and should be done regularly. Thinning trees and shrubs will promote the growth of younger, healthier branches, which rejuvenates the plant.

Early spring is the single best time to prune. Most woody ornamentals need some annual pruning, and for gardeners itching to do some "real" gardening, this is the chore that fits the bill. For all but a few of the woody components of the landscape, the best time to prune them is when they are dormant. That means that pruning should occur after the leaves fall and

142

before they bud out in spring. However, pruning in spring is the best possible time because any damage that is done through the pruning process will be quickly remedied by rapid spring growth.

Trees and shrubs that flower before June should be pruned after they have flowered. Trees and shrubs that flower after June can be pruned in spring. Don't prune trees or shrubs when growth has started and buds are swelling. Prune before growth starts in spring or wait until plants have leafed out.

Necessary tools include a good-quality pair of secateurs and loppers and a medium-sized pruning saw. Good quality pruning tools make a big job so much easier. Regardless of the quality of your tools, always ensure they are clean and sharp; clean tools will help prevent spreading disease.

Use the correct tool for the size of branch to be removed when pruning: secateurs, or hand pruners, for growth up to 2.5 cm (1") in diameter; long-handled loppers for growth up to 5 cm (2") in diameter; or a pruning saw for growth up to about 15 cm (6") in diameter.

Don't leave stubs when pruning. Whether you are cutting off a large branch or deadheading a lilac, always cut back to a joint. Branches should be removed to the branch collar, and smaller growth should be cut back to a bud or branch union.

There is no absolute set angle for pruning. **Each plant should be pruned according to its individual needs.**

Never use pruning paint or paste. Trees have a natural ability to create a barrier between living and dead wood. Painting over a cut impairs this ability. Instead, learn to prune properly and always prune at the best time to ensure the best healing of your valuable trees and shrubs.

Never try to remove a tree, large branch or branches growing near power lines or other hazardous areas by yourself, especially if they could damage a building, fence or car if they were to fall. Have someone help you, or hire a professional, such as someone certified by the International Society of Arborists (ISA). Branches and trees are usually much heavier than anticipated and can do a lot of damage if they fall in the wrong place.

Trees

Many types of shade trees need only minimal pruning. **Prune off dead, diseased or dying branches and any growth that is out of bounds.**

Evergreens can be pruned once the new growth has fully extended, but while it is still tender. This new growth is called a candle. Each candle can be pinched back by up to half to encourage bushier growth. Never cut evergreens back into old wood because most of them cannot regenerate from old wood.

Avoid pruning rust-prone plants such as mountain ash and crab apple in late summer and fall because many rusts are releasing spores at the end of the growing season. Trees with open cut wounds are especially vulnerable.

Hedges

Begin training hedge plants when they are very young. To train a hedge properly, you have to cut the plants back quite severely while they are small to ensure they branch out to form dense growth.

Formal hedges are generally sheared at least twice per growing season, and they are trimmed more severely than informal hedges to assume a neat, even appearance.

Informal hedges take advantage of the natural shape of the plants and require only minimal trimming.

These hedges generally take up more room than formal hedges. Informal hedges are pretty if you choose to plant flowering or fruiting shrubs. Lilacs or hardy shrub roses are great choices for hedges and are not used enough in this manner.

For any hedge, trim all sides to encourage even growth. The base of your hedge should always be wider than the top to allow light to reach the entire hedge and to prevent it from thinning out at the base. Trim hedges regularly to keep them looking tidy and lush.

During winter when the snow gets heavy, an improperly pruned hedge will collapse under the weight of the snow. When this happens, the hedge must be rejuvenated by cutting it back severely to allow the base to expand.

Propagating

There are two types of propagation. Sexual propagation is basically the production of seed. Most annuals and biennials are produced by seed. To grow perennials by seed is often a bit more challenging, and usually it will take more than one year from starting the seed to produce some flowers. Asexual propagation is a way to produce more plants without having to grow them from seed. They are genetically identical to the parent plant. There are many kinds of asexual propagation, some of which are relatively easy while others can be more difficult.

Some plants are easy to propagate—strawberries, for example. Peg down the runners either into an open spot in the soil near the mother plant, or into a small container. Cut the runner when the daughter plants have rooted and are exhibiting new growth.

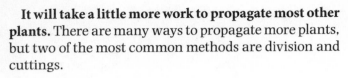

It will take a little more work to propagate most other plants. There are many ways to propagate more plants, but two of the most common methods are division and cuttings.

Division

Most perennials will eventually need to be divided. The plants themselves will provide signs that it is time to be divided. It is time when the centre of the plant has died out or when the plant is no longer flowering as profusely as it did in previous years. It is also necessary when the plant is encroaching on the growing space of other plants. **Divide perennials that bloom in mid-summer or later, such as asters, daylilies and sedums, in early spring. Divide spring-blooming perennials in fall.**

Think about the size the plant was when you first got it or how big similar plants are at the garden centre, and try to make your plant divisions about that size. Depending on the size of your perennials, you can divide them using a shovel or pitchfork (for large plants), a sharp knife (for small plants) or your hands (for easily divided plants).

To divide tubers and rhizomes, separate or cut them into sections, but be aware that each section needs to have a segment of the crown with at least one eye or bud.

Replant divisions as soon as possible. Extra divisions can be spread around into other areas of the garden, shared with friends or composted.

Cuttings

Taking cuttings involves removing a piece from a parent plant that will regrow the lost tissues and is a great way to grow more of your favourite shrubs for yourself and your gardening friends. **The easiest**

cuttings to take from woody plants such as trees, shrubs and vines are called softwood stem cuttings. They are taken from mature new growth that has not yet become completely woody, usually in mid- to late summer. Hardy shrub roses will reproduce easily by cuttings such as these. Hardwood stem cuttings are taken from tissue that has already become woody.

Take softwood cuttings from healthy shoots that are not flowering and have not yet become woody. Take cuttings that are 5–10 cm (2–4") in length. Always make stem cuttings just below a leaf node, the point where the leaves are attached to the stem. Remove the lower leaves, but leave a couple of leaves at the top of the cutting. Fill a container with peat moss or compost and firmly pack it. Place the cuttings in the container with the leaves above the surface of the planting medium. Label the cuttings and keep them warm and moist. Once they have rooted, place them in individual pots, and plant them out once the container is filled with new, healthy roots.

Take hardwood cuttings anytime after a killing frost until late winter. Take a cutting that is 15–30 cm (6–12") long and make the cut at an angle. Bury the cutting in moist vermiculite or sand. In spring, plant the cutting in a hot bed or other protected site, leaving a few centimetres of the cutting above ground.

Take leaf cuttings from plants such as African violet, begonia and many other succulents. The procedure is similar to stem cuttings. Insert about one-third of a leaf into the planting medium. Make small cuts in the leaf where it is touching the medium. It is at these points that new growth will occur.

Take root cuttings during the dormant season to ensure the carbohydrate level in the root is high. Cut straight through the end of the root nearest the stem

and cut the other end on a slant. Store the cuttings for about three weeks in rooting medium at 5° C (40° F), and then plant them in a warm, bright location. If you need to take the cuttings during a period of active growth, simply skip the storage period and plant them directly in a warm, bright place.

Other Methods of Propagation

Layering will cause roots to develop on shoots that are still attached to the parent plant and is a great propagation method for vines. To do simple layering, take a branch and place it on the ground. Scrape the bark a little bit near the end, and put that part of the branch underground. Place a small rock on that spot. Within a few weeks, roots will have formed. Once there are sufficient roots, simply cut the branch between the spot where the new roots formed and the parent plant and plant your cutting in the location of choice.

Grafting is to join segments of two different plants of the same species. **For grafting to be successful, the cambium layers must be aligned.** This process is used to produce earlier fruiting or to create different culti-vars on the same plant. Imagine having an apple tree that would produce a few different types of apples.

A similar technique is called budding. In this proce-dure, a single bud is added to the host plant. **Budding is usually easier than grafting; when budding, you do not have to have cambium tissues aligned.**

Watering

Watering Basics

Water is often the only limiting factor in plant growth. If Mother Nature does not provide enough water, then the gardener must provide it. **Get a rain gauge to measure how much water nature is providing.** If you are receiving 2.5 cm (1") of water a week, then additional watering is not likely needed. A rain gauge can be a fancy commercial type or a can (tuna, cat food, etc.) with straight sides that is monitored and emptied at least weekly when you've been getting rain.

Your water outlets and hoses should be able to reach all parts of your garden that need watering. You may need to install extra water hoses or water lines for ease of access and use throughout the growing season.

Water your trees, shrubs and perennials in spring if spring rain or snow melt has not provided enough moisture. Water your lawn and garden beds in summer, but no more than once a week during dry spells. **Check the root zone before watering.** The soil surface may appear dry when the roots are still moist.

Water deeply, slowly and thoroughly. Deep, infrequent watering encourages deep, strong roots. Frequent, shallow watering will cause roots to grow only in the upper soil layer (where the water is). These shallow-rooted plants will not be able to tolerate any drought.

New transplants of trees, shrubs and perennials need to be watered regularly to help them establish themselves and to reduce transplant shock, especially if the weather is hot and dry. Monitor your new transplants while their root systems are becoming established. Wilt may occur if the roots can't keep up with how much water the foliage is transpiring. A technique known as syringing will provide the plants with the relief they need. Simply turn on a sprinkler for five minutes or so to increase the humidity around the plant.

The best time to water is early in the morning before 9:00 AM, especially when wind conditions are calm. Morning watering minimizes evaporation losses and also minimizes the amount of time the foliage remains wet, which reduces the incidence of fungal diseases. The next best time is at dusk. Check to see if your municipality or county has any watering restrictions.

Powdery mildew and other fungal diseases can be reduced by watering the soil under the plant rather than watering from above and wetting the foliage. A good soaker hose or a drip irrigation system work well for that purpose. Water is delivered to the base of the plant in a slow trickle, eliminating any moisture on the foliage and reducing moisture lost through evaporation.

Water-Saving Tips

Water-wise landscapes are those that contain plants that are adapted to the local climate and environment so that they will only need supplemental water during establishment and during prolonged drought periods. **Look to nature as your guide to selecting appropriate plants for your landscape and garden.**

For efficient maintenance and watering, group plants together that have similar cultural requirements. Do not attempt to grow plants with dissimilar watering needs in the same area—one plant or the other will suffer.

When you increase the amount of organic matter in the soil, you increase the soil's ability to hold water. This is a real benefit in areas that are hot and dry or that experience occasional drought.

Do not water your garden according to a schedule. Water only when your plants need it. This prevents overwatering and saves money on your utility bill.

Rainwater is a valuable resource. **Harvest the rain as it falls by directing the rainfall to the areas that you choose using drainspouts and hoses, or collect rainwater for use in the garden during dry spells.** Cover the rain barrel with a screen to exclude insects.

Set up your sprinklers so that they are watering only the garden or landscape plants and not your patio or sidewalk, and use a timer. A lot of water can be wasted if you forget there is a sprinkler running. Make sure that your hoses or irrigation system do not have any leaks or obstructions.

Closely monitor your landscape when watering to ensure that the water is penetrating into the soil and not running off. If you notice water run-off or water pooling on the surface, discontinue watering until the soil has had a chance to absorb the water already applied. It may be that you have to apply 1 cm (½") of water, wait a couple hours, then apply another 1 cm (½") of water.

Weeding

A weed in the garden is any plant that is growing in a location you do not want it to grow. Weeds take up valuable space and compete with your other plants for nutrients, water and light.

Weeding is unfortunately an essential chore in the garden. **If you get rid of the weeds in your beds when you see them and they are small, you can avoid having to spend an entire day doing it later.** Eradicate those weeds when they are small—before they spread and produce seeds. Once the weeds are gone, surface mulch will help prevent future growth.

Recreational Weeding

Remove weeds by good, old-fashioned digging. Be sure to remove as much of the root system as possible because a whole new plant can start if you miss even a small portion of the roots or underground stems. Getting the entire weed, root and all, can be an almost impossible task if your ground is dry and hard, so take some time to pull weeds after it has rained or after irrigation.

Use the correct tool for the job. If you are trying to pull a weed with a long tap root such as the lovely dandelion, use a long tool with a V-shaped end to help loosen the soil at the end of the tap root. For weeds with shallow root systems, scrape the soil with a sharp hoe to attempt to drag the weed and the root from the soil. If you have a bad back, use a tool with a long handle to minimize the time you have to bend.

Weeds often grow between the cracks in the patio, pavement or deck. **Use a sharp, narrow blade with a 90° angle to easily take care of this problem.** Boiling water is also a good solution to weeds that are hard to get. Pour boiling water over the weeds to kill them. Use the blade to get those that did not succumb to the scalding.

Extreme Weeding

You may decide that you need some extra help of a chemical nature. Glyphosate is a non-selective product that will kill any plant it touches. If you have inherited a property that has a huge weed problem, then sometimes, to get control of the problem initially, you might choose to pull out the big guns. **If you do choose to use a chemical product, it is important to closely follow the manufacturer's directions.**

Full-strength household vinegar has been shown to be effective at killing a number of different weeds, especially on a hot, sunny day. Higher concentration garden vinegars are becoming commercially available specifically for use against weeds. Be aware that vinegar is non-selective and can kill or injure most plants. Vinegar will also lower the pH of the soil, but usually only temporarily.

Solarization is an effective way of removing stubborn weeds. Till the area and remove debris and large clods. Ensure the soil is moist. Cover the area with a thick sheet of clear plastic, tucking in the edges. Leave the plastic in place for one to two months. The existing vegetation will be killed, along with many of the seeds in the soil seed bank. However, this process also favours the development of anaerobic soil microorganisms, which can be dealt with later in the soil preparation process.

Weeds can be starved to death. **Starvation methods deplete the carbohydrate reserve in the weeds' root systems but can take a whole season to be effective.** The first method is to remove all the top growth, till the area, wait for new top growth to appear and then repeat the whole process. However, the increased tilling will lower the soil microorganism population. The second method is to remove the top growth of the weeds, wait until new growth appears and then repeat the process. Removing the top growth is easily accomplished with a hoe. The young top growth can be added to your compost pile.

Sizzweeding uses a hot flame to damage the top growth of a weed. Sizzweeding does not pollute the soil, but it does pollute the air. **Flame weeding is most effective when the flame is passed briefly over the plant.** This damages the foliage, and the plant uses up a lot of energy reserves trying to repair the damage. Completely frying the top growth to a crisp makes it easy for the plant to send up new leaves.

Sometimes, the introduction of exotic or alien plant species becomes an invasion because there are no natural checks in the new area to limit the spread. **In cases like these, biological controls such as weed eaters are often effective when traditional methods of control are not.** Weed eaters control pest weeds by feeding on all plant parts. They are specific to only one plant species, are prolific and colonize well. However, they will sometimes be a complete failure as a solution if they are unable to establish in the new location for whatever reason.

Fertilizing

Fertilization is essential to plant health. Nutrients naturally occur in the soil, but depending on the health of your soil, you may be lacking some essential nutrients for plant growth. Nine macronutrients and seven micronutrients are essential for optimum plant growth. An insufficient amount of any of these elements will result in your plants not growing as well as they could.

Organic vs. Inorganic

There are two broad types of fertilizers: organic and inorganic. Organic fertilizers are derived from living plant or animal sources and are relatively expensive. Inorganic fertilizers are synthetic and are generally less expensive than organic fertilizers. **The plants do not recognize the difference between organic or inorganic nutrients; however, once the fertilizer is added to the soil, inorganic nutrients are generally available to the plants instantly, while organic nutrients will be available to the plants slowly and steadily over time.**

Always try to use organic means of fertilizing, such as compost, avoiding chemicals altogether. If compost is scarce or unavailable, try to use an organic fertilizer rather than a synthetic product. Both types of fertilizers are made of chemicals, but the organic chemicals will break down over time, whereas the inorganic chemicals will not.

Fertilizing Tips

The timing of fertilization in the landscape is critical. **Fertilize very early in spring, prior to any real growth occurring.** Fertilizing your landscape once a year is usually adequate. However, high-rainfall areas might require an application twice a year.

There are always times that specific plants may need a boost of fertilizer. When planting bulbs, add a little bone meal to the soil to encourage root development. When transplanting, always water in the plant with a dilute high-phosphorus fertilizer solution.

Some plants may need multiple applications, but always reduce fertilizer applications in late summer or early fall, depending on the region, to allow perennials, shrubs and trees ample time to harden off before the cold weather. Too much fertilizer encourages the plants to continue to grow rapidly and therefore not prepare for the winter season.

Plant-Specific Maintenance

Lawns

Aerate your lawn in spring, after active growth begins, to relieve compaction and to allow water and air to move freely through the soil.

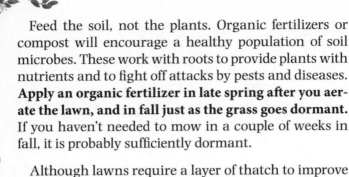

Feed the soil, not the plants. Organic fertilizers or compost will encourage a healthy population of soil microbes. These work with roots to provide plants with nutrients and to fight off attacks by pests and diseases. **Apply an organic fertilizer in late spring after you aerate the lawn, and in fall just as the grass goes dormant.** If you haven't needed to mow in a couple of weeks in fall, it is probably sufficiently dormant.

Although lawns require a layer of thatch to improve wear tolerance, reduce compaction and insulate against weather extremes, too thick a thatch layer can prevent water absorption, make the grass susceptible to heat, drought and cold and encourage pest and disease problems. **De-thatch lawns in spring only when the thatch layer is more than 2 cm (¾") deep.**

Mow lawns to a height of 5–6 cm (2–2½"). If kept this height, the remaining leaf blade will shade the ground, which will prevent moisture loss, keep the roots cool, reduce the stress the grass suffers from being mowed and help the grass out-compete weeds for space and sunlight.

Leave grass clippings on the lawn to return their nutrients to the soil and add organic matter. Mowing your lawn once a week or as often as needed during the vigorous growing season will ensure that the clippings decompose quickly.

Healthy turfgrass will out-compete most weeds. **Remove weeds by hand. If you must use chemicals, apply them only to the weeds.** Chemical herbicides disrupt the balance of soil microbes and are not necessary to have a healthy lawn.

Lawns need very little water to remain green. **Water deeply and infrequently to encourage deep roots that are not easily damaged during periods of drought.** Grass can be kept alive with 0.5 cm (¼") of water a week, and 2.5 cm (1") a week will keep it green.

Seed areas of the lawn that are thin or dead in spring or fall. Cool fall weather is ideal for sowing grass seed and repairing thin patches in the lawn. Keep the seed well-watered while it germinates.

Keep off your lawn when it is frozen, bare of snow and/or very wet to avoid damaging the grass or compacting the soil.

Tender Bulbs

Summer-flowering bulbs are quite wonderful, but they are tender and require a little bit more work than spring-flowering bulbs. You might think that it is worth every bit of trouble to grow some of these beauties that need to be lifted in order to survive our winter temperatures. Storage is really quite simple. Once your area has received a killing frost, the foliage of the tender, summer-flowering bulbs will have frozen. This is the time to lift those bulbs and prepare them for storage. Don't wait until temperatures are cold enough to kill the bulb altogether.

Canna lilies grace many public areas in less severe climates for a number of reasons. **They are spectacular while in bloom, and the foliage is often quite beautiful on its own. They are also a really easy keeper with very few problems.** After a killing frost, trim the stems to a few centimetres from the rhizomes. Lift the rhizomes and store them in slightly damp peat moss at about 10° C (50° F). Check periodically that the peat has not completely dried; if it is dry, dampen it slightly.

Calla lilies are equally as beautiful and always worth growing. After a killing frost, cut the foliage back to a few centimetres and let the bulbs cure for a couple of weeks. Store them at about 5° C (40° F).

Gladiolas are a spectacular flower to grow. Lift the corms about six weeks after flowering and remove the stalk down to about 5 cm (2"). If you had thrip damage during the year, soak the corms in 15° C (60° F) water or in a dilute bleach solution for a few minutes to kill the little blighters. Dry the corms fully and remove the oldest bottom corm. Store them at about 2° C (35° F).

Tuberous begonias are one of the few plants that have the ability to look spectacular in full shade areas. They bring a tropical hue to your garden and are easy to store over winter. After a killing frost, carefully lift the tubers and remove most of the stem. Let them dry in a well-ventilated area, and once the stems are fully dry, they are easy to remove. Store the tubers in peat moss at about 5° C (40° F). Check periodically to ensure they are not getting soft or mouldy.

Dahlias have so much variety in colour and size that they can be used throughout the landscape. Carefully lift the cluster of tubers and remove the top growth after a killing frost. Wash the extra soil off and dry the tubers for a few hours. Store them in peat moss at about 5° C (40° F) and check occasionally to be sure they do not dry out completely.

Check tubers or bulbs in storage over winter to see how they are doing. It may be necessary to add a bit of moisture to the medium in which they are stored if that specific bulb needs to be stored moist. Some tubers or bulbs may start to decay over the storage period, so if you notice softness or mould beginning, discard those bulbs. If any have started sprouting, pot them and keep them in a bright location.

Water Garden Plants

A thorough cleanout in spring gets your pond ready for the growing season. This involves removing your fish and looking after any eggs or tadpoles of frogs and other amphibians, pumping or bailing out the water, scooping or pumping out any accumulated debris, hosing the rocks off a bit, cleaning the filters, replacing worn filter parts and adding fresh water. Not all ponds will need this level of cleaning annually, but a spring cleaning is a great opportunity to give your plants a little tender loving care.

Clear any dead plants out of the pond. If you aren't sure if a plant is dead, you can always trim back any growth you think is dead and make a note to check back in a few weeks, when the water has warmed a little more.

Push slow-release fertilizer tabs into the soil around your aquatic plants, particularly around heavy feeders such as water lilies and lotus plants, according to the package directions. Also in spring, you can work compost into the soil around your pondside plants to improve the soil without worrying about excess nutrients washing into the pond, which often happens with chemical fertilizers.

One thing that many pond plants have in common is vigorous growth. This vigorous growth can quickly fill your pond and throw your ecosystem out of balance. **A certain amount of trimming and pruning may be required to keep the growth from swamping your pond.** Regular trimming will also reduce the amount of material decomposing in your pond. Decomposing material produces gases that can be harmful to fish, beneficial bacteria and some of the important insects and amphibians in your pond.

As the nights begin to get colder and the first frost is expected, get your pond ready for winter. Most water plants will die back completely in fall; remove as much of the dead or dying vegetation as you can to avoid having it decompose in the water. Most tropical plants

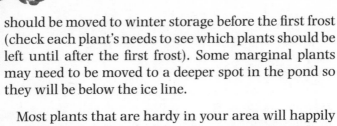

should be moved to winter storage before the first frost (check each plant's needs to see which plants should be left until after the first frost). Some marginal plants may need to be moved to a deeper spot in the pond so they will be below the ice line.

Most plants that are hardy in your area will happily overwinter right in the pond. In most of our gardens, ponds over 45 cm (18") deep will only partially freeze. **Having some of the pond remain unfrozen gives plants (as well as fish, amphibians and any other pond dwellers) the best chance to survive winter.**

Container Garden Plants

To keep the plants in your containers blooming, ensure you are providing enough water and food. Using good-quality compost as a top dressing for the container allows the nutrients from the compost to filter down into the potting mix with each watering.

Planted containers can dry out quickly, especially on a hot summer day. To check for moisture, look at the soil surface; if it is dry, then lift the container (if it is not too large). If the container feels light, then you need to water. You can also poke your finger into the potting mix to see how dry the root zone is.

Container plants are most attractive if they are fertilized throughout the growing season. Some gardeners choose to use a dilute liquid fertilizer solution each time they water. Otherwise, fertilize every two weeks during the growing season. Using a slow-release fertilizer at planting time is a labour saver. Top dress your containers with the recommended amount at planting time, and you will have enough fertilizer for up to three months.

Most perennials, shrubs or trees in containers will require more winter protection than they would if grown in the ground. Because the roots are above ground level, they are exposed to the winter wind and freeze and thaw cycles. Protect container-grown plants by insulating the inside of the container. Thin sheets of foam insulation can be purchased and fitted around the inside of the pot before the soil is added.

Move containers with tender plants to a sheltered location over winter. Garden sheds and unheated garages work well to protect plants from the cold and wind.

Critters

All gardens are shared with animals. Many gardeners have pets, but even if they don't, there will always be wildlife about. Keep the critters in mind when you are planning and working in your garden.

Pets and the Garden

When planning your garden with pets in mind, remember that anything out of place sticks out, drawing your attention to it. **Informal garden settings tend to lend themselves better to pets.**

Your pets will appreciate creature comforts in the garden just as they do in your home. Pets will need a shady location to hang out, eat and drink, particularly during those hot days of summer. A fresh bowl of water will help keep your pets out of puddles and the water garden.

Consider an elevated platform for your pets to rest on. It will allow them a vantage point from which to survey their domain.

Keeping Pets In or Out

Pet-friendly gardens always have a good fence protecting pets from escaping, which will keep them from the dangers that lurk outside the comfort of their backyard. A fence at least 1.2 m (4') high will be enough for some pets, particularly small dogs. A taller fence will be needed to keep larger and more athletic dogs and cats inside the yard. Fences reaching 1.5–1.8 m (5–6') heights will usually suffice. A fenced yard can add an architectural quality to your landscape while protecting your pet and plants.

Gaps in a fence can be problematic for curious pets that can wedge their heads into the gaps or even sneak through to the other side. Gaps along the bottom can also be a problem, enabling dogs to dig their way out. **Chicken wire or wire mesh can be used to fill or block gaps, preventing your pets from getting stuck.**

The entire garden or yard may not have to be fenced in. **A dog run may be adequate for your canine. A cat enclosure in your garden will prevent your feline from roaming too far.** Both enclosures contain the area in which your pet can roam within the garden and can be designed to blend into the garden rather than being an eyesore or standalone. Products are available at your local pet store, hardware store, online retailer or mail order supplier to build such a structure. A landscape designer or architect can supply you with tips to camouflage it amongst the greenery, which will also benefit your pet on those hot, sunny days. Provide water, shelter, somewhere soft to sleep, a litter box and food to make the enclosure comfortable.

If you separate your plants from your pet, you can grow any plant you choose without the potential of your pet damaging your plants and/or getting ill from inadvertently chewing a plant or two. Simple fencing can prevent pets from soiling, digging or chewing up your vegetable, herb or flower gardens. To ensure the safety of sensitive, tender or tiny plants, try a temporary chicken wire enclosure to keep your pets out.

Leave a wide enough gap along your fence and garden to allow your dog to run alongside the fence. This will prevent him from running through your garden.

Raised beds are ideal for keeping pets, particularly dogs, out of flower and vegetable gardens. The height of the beds is determined by the height of the dog. Small breeds won't bother with beds 30–60 cm (12–24") tall, while larger breeds will be kept out of taller beds 60 cm

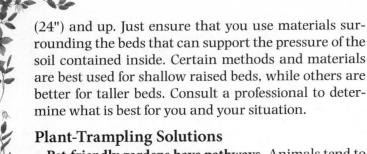

(24") and up. Just ensure that you use materials surrounding the beds that can support the pressure of the soil contained inside. Certain methods and materials are best used for shallow raised beds, while others are better for taller beds. Consult a professional to determine what is best for you and your situation.

Plant-Trampling Solutions

Pet-friendly gardens have pathways. Animals tend to beeline to a particular destination, and they habitually take the same path every day. Worn-out dirt trails in the lawn aren't very attractive and are easily preventable by building a path with stepping stones, pavers, crushed gravel, sidewalk blocks, bark mulch or a hardy, tough groundcover. Small cedar chips are easy on paws yet large enough to resist clinging to soft and silky coats.

Paths made from rock, gravel, concrete, pavers or bricks are often the most practical and appropriate. Playful dogs can sometimes disturb loose material in paths of soil, mulch or other soft materials, all of which will also be tracked into the house by little muddy paws on wet days.

If soft or loose pathways are your preference, regardless of the potential for tracking in dirt and mud, install a hard surface right outside the door your pets use to go in and out. Placing a large mat on the hard surface will reduce the amount of mud, grass and moisture tracked into the house.

Use driftwood along pathways to persuade dogs to stay away from planted areas on the other side, while beautifying the area at the same time.

Plants chosen for along pathways should be selected not only for their beauty, light, soil and moisture requirements, but also for their sturdiness, at least where dogs are concerned. The foliage should be soft but sturdy enough to stand some doggie roughhousing.

When trying to prevent animals from going into or through certain areas of the garden, plant densely and wisely. Mass shrubs and ornamental grasses together to ensure that the pets travel around rather than through the area in question. Grasses are particularly tough plants and are even strong enough to withstand any damage that may come about with rambunctious dogs. Prickly, thorny and spiny plants are recommended by some people but can cause serious eye injuries, so be aware of the possibilities.

When trying to spruce up an area of your lawn, sod is the best bet. Seed may take too long to germinate, at least when there's a dog or cat milling about.

Digging Solutions

Having bare soil in a garden is like inviting your pets to dig right in, and we mean literally. **Plant perennials close together and choose pet-friendly plants, ones that can tolerate some abuse.** Groundcovers such as thyme, spreading cotoneaster, sweet woodruff and periwinkle provide enough coverage to discourage your cats and dogs from digging in your beds. Inorganic mulches such as gravel may be best for areas where your pets are insistent when it comes to their digging habits.

When seeding vegetable gardens, try to keep the soil moist, particularly when the seed is germinating. Cats prefer to dig in dry and loose soil, so moist soil will likely act as a deterrent.

Mulch the soil between the rows of your vegetables. Straw is a great mulch to cover the soil along pathways in the vegetable garden, and most critters will not dig into it.

Keep the compost heap out of the reach of both cats and dogs. Your pooch may dig into it for something to eat, while your kitty may feel compelled to use it as a litter box.

Dogs tend to imitate what they see, so hanging around their owner who's digging in the garden might be understood as a lesson on digging. **Ensure that your dogs have entertainment of their own while you're sharing the space outdoors.**

Dogs are often curious about what humans have just buried in the garden and respond by digging it up. Not only can this be a nuisance, but it also can be dangerous; some bulbs are toxic or poisonous to dogs. **Either avoid bulbs that may make them sick, or keep your bulb planting from your dogs so they don't even know that the bulbs are there.**

When all else fails, provide a spot for your dog to dig that is all his own. Fill a children's wading pool with sand or dig a small pit and fill it with soil or sand. Take your dog out and let her see you bury a few of her toys and treats. Bury new ones from time to time. Teach your dog that the people's garden is not a good place to dig, but the dog's garden is.

Pet Safety

When pets have access to the yard and garden, it's imperative that they're not exposed to any dangers. **Whenever possible, choose alternatives to pesticides, herbicides and fertilizers.** Non-toxic alternatives exist and are available at your local garden centre; if they're not, then suggest that it carry them.

Be careful with any type of chemical usage—fertilizers, pesticides and herbicides—in your garden, even organic products. Many can harm or kill pets, so take the time to research the products you plan on using before the seal is ever broken. If you do use a product that is toxic to animals, take a few precautions to protect your pets, including removing all food and water bowls from the area, or anything your pets might drink out of for that matter, before you spray or apply the product. Keep them out of the garden until the treated areas are safe once again, based on the product's recommendations. This is usually once the product is dry or after a period of 24 hours, but check the label and instructions to be sure.

If slugs are a problem in your garden, stay away from any of the older types of slug bait that contain metaldehyde, which is harmful to pets when ingested. Slug bait made with the active ingredient iron phosphate is a much safer alternative, but it's still best to prevent your pets from entering the treated areas until the product is rendered innocuous by either time, water or formulation.

Many organic amendments often found in fertilizers, such as bone meal, blood meal or fish emulsion, can be very attractive to a curious dog or cat. **Keep all chemicals, even organically based chemicals and amendments, in sealed containers with secure lids and in their original packaging.** If you ever have to refer back to the packaging to determine how to treat a pet (or human) who has ingested the product, you'll find yourself lost and in a panic if the packaging has been disposed of. Or, store such products in areas your pets (and children) cannot gain access to.

Keep plants that are toxic to animals out of the garden if you have pets that spend time in the yard. Although most pets aren't likely to start chewing on your plants, some might, particularly young pets. Avoid plants such as rhubarb, lily-of-the-valley, azalea and hydrangea. There are others, of course, and it's best to do a little research prior to planting to find out which plants could possibly harm your pets. There is a world of information both in reference books and online.

Don't let your pets out while mowing the lawn or when using other power tools in the garden. Their curiosity can sometimes put them in dangerous situations.

Don't leave sharp tools where pets can step on them, particularly grafting knives and the like. Periodically check the yard and garden for sharp or rusted objects and remove any you find to prevent your pets from getting injured.

Cocoa bean mulch isn't commonly found yet, but it is gaining in popularity in varied regions throughout the country. Compared to other species, dogs are particularly sensitive to a substance called theobromine that is found in cocoa beans. This is the same substance found in chocolate that, when ingested, will cause your dog to become ill. **Avoid cocoa bean mulch or products that include this product in dog-friendly yards and gardens.** Other mulching alternatives exist that are safer for your dog, including bark mulch, chopped fall leaves, grass clippings and pine needles.

When staking plants such as small trees in the yard where your dogs are allowed to play and roam, avoid invisible wires or supports that they might run into. Thicker, soft, visible ties are recommended to prevent injury.

Look around for small spaces where curious pets may get stuck. This includes under a deck or behind a shed.

Ponds, although beautiful, can be harmful to some pets. **Ensure that your pets can climb out of your pond if they were ever to jump or fall in.** Build steps or staggered edges around the perimeter of your pond to allow your pets to step out, rather than a slippery, sloped edge that will prevent them from getting the foothold necessary to escape. Even large dogs can drown if they are trapped in a pond.

Dog Business

Consider selecting a specific marker, such as a piece of driftwood, for your pup to mark his territory—a "lift-your-leg" post, if you will. Not only will it beautify the space, but it will also reduce the number of locations where your dog is compelled to urinate. With a little training and consistent, friendly reminders, this will be the one and only focus of his leg-lifting, saving a myriad of plants.

There is no truth to the belief that female dog urine causes more damage to lawns because of its caustic and acidic nature. Dog urine can damage lawns, shrubs and perennials because of the concentrated nitrogen, which can burn plants, but this is true of both sexes. **Train your dog to urinate in a designated area where plants won't be affected or where you care little for the plants.**

Don't believe that adding tomato juice, baking soda or salt to your dog's diet will reduce the damage to plants caused by urine. Such things will only make your dog sick and may increase the risk of bladder disease and other serious health problems. Training is the only solution; designate a location where the dog can urinate.

If your dog does any of his business on the lawn, clean it up often. Remove any poop frequently and run a sprinkler occasionally to wash away odours and urine. Diluting the urine will also lessen any burning; in fact, it will green up the spot where it occurred. Any animal will begin to avoid the "toilet" if it's filthy, causing them to go in places you may later regret. And what's worse than having to clean up a winter's worth of poop in early spring?

If the dog in your life and lawns simply do not go together, create a special potty area where she's allowed

to do her business. Cover the area with wood chips or pea gravel (excuse the pun) and screen it from view with a trellis, fence or grouping of plants. Dogs prefer an absorbent surface.

Make sure that all dog poop goes into the garbage or down the toilet. Do not put any feces into the compost pile—ever. It could contain worms or other hazards that won't be remedied by a stint in the compost heap.

More Dog Tips

Bored dogs are more likely to get into trouble, just like children. Use walks and games to burn up your dog's excess energy, rather than your dog using that energy for destructive behaviour when you're not around. If your dog is tempted to treat small plants like chew toys, particularly small trees and shrubs, plant older specimens that are not as easily damaged.

Make the choice as to where your dog is allowed to go and be consistent. It won't help your training endeavours if you allow your pooch to go into the garden when it's weedy but expect him to respect the same space after you've cleaned it all up.

Encourage behaviour you approve of and discourage behaviour you don't approve of regarding your dog's actions in the garden. Use verbal clues such as "out of the garden" to keep her out of garden beds.

Your dog is bound to want to be where you are, so take him with you for a portion of the time you're in the garden. If your focus is simply on the garden and not on him, then put him inside or take him for a walk, rather than wonder why he's digging a hole in your lawn to get your attention.

Lonely, singular plants are more vulnerable to damage from playful doggie romps than large clumps of plants. Plant large groups of perennials so that even if your dog gets carried away and takes one or two plants out, you still have plenty left to admire.

If you are starting from scratch and designing a garden with plans for your dog to share the same space, try to implement your pooch into the design. For example, if your dog likes to run on a circular path around the house, then planting a hedge as a blockade is sure to spell failure. If your dog is determined to run rampant through a particular portion of your garden, even a location where you want to plant something, then you may as well let him. One gardener planted lavender along her fence where her dogs liked to run and play. The lavender was unscathed, and the dogs came inside every day smelling of lavender. If you can't beat them, join them.

Cat Tips

Integrate an outdoor scratching post where cats know it's all right to sharpen up their little claws. They will appreciate a place where they're allowed to scratch and claw.

Cats are bound to use some part of the yard as an outdoor litter box. **Train them to use only one small part of the yard once you've chosen an out-of-sight location.**

Avoid planting any species from the Nepeta family, which includes catnip and catmint, if you're trying to discourage neighbourhood feline visitors. Although the plants are tough and tolerant of being rolled upon and eaten, you may not be as tolerant of cats other than your own visiting your garden.

When designing a pond, consider that cats will take advantage of the ease of entry to catch any fish. This can be prevented by growing a border of plants around the perimeter or creating some other barrier to keep your cat out. Add fish only to ponds that have limited or no access at all, at least for your cat.

Lay chicken wire over freshly seeded beds to prevent your kitty from thinking they were recently dug and manicured for her. Cats dislike the feeling of the wire on the pads of their paws. The chicken wire can remain on the surface of the soil until the seeds germinate. When the seedlings come up, gently remove the wire and replace it with either netting, a fence or a thick layer of mulch. Once the plants are larger and established, the protection can be removed.

Wildlife and the Garden

It is always a pleasure to see wildlife in your landscape. With the rapid rate of urban sprawl, wildlife has experienced a significant loss of habitat, but we can provide some of the space, shelter, food and water that wildlife needs in our gardens. **Although you may not want to attract every creature, you can make at least some wildlife welcome in your garden.**

The first step to becoming a wildlife gardener is to determine what critters you wish to attract. It is then necessary to find out what to plant to attract the forms of animal life that you want without the ones you don't want.

Attracting Wildlife in General

If you want to attract wildlife, there are a few basic principles that can be applied to a landscape of any size.

- **There must be diversity.** The more diverse your landscape plants are, the more diverse and beneficial wildlife you will attract. Find space for lawns, flower beds, low shrubs, hedges, taller shrubs and trees.

- **There must be a balance between lawn and taller vegetation.** Only half of the available space in the yard should be turf. Place low plants beside the lawn and plant progressively taller plants behind those. Gradually move the ceiling taller by planting low shrubs, taller shrubs and finally small and large trees.

- **There must be a balance between evergreen and deciduous trees and shrubs.** Choose species that hold their fruit and/or seeds well so that there is available food for late winter and early spring, and that provide shelter on those cold, windy winter days. Plant groups of assorted evergreen and deciduous trees and shrubs together, with only a short distance between the groups.

- **Open space is important for letting in sunlight and providing the "edge effect" that is essential for good nesting habitat.** Along the edge is where most flowers are seen in bloom and where fruits and berries ripen most luxuriantly. The largest number of bees, butterflies and day-flying moths are also found along the edge. Border all openings with an appropriate assortment of plants. A simple way to create a border is to leave an area of lawn uncut. A border can be created between an area of mowed lawn and an area of lawn that is uncut. Another border can be created between the lawn and an area planted with a groundcover.

- **The yard should be neat but not manicured.** Do not prune hedges too vigorously, or they will become impenetrable. Heavy pruning also removes blossoms and fruit buds, hence a food source. Judicious pruning improves the appearance of shrubs and trees as well as shelter and nesting potentials. Leave old trees if they are healthy. Let vines crawl over the old, dead trees to improve their appearance. Create a wild area in your garden. It can be as simple as leaving a pile of branches in an unused corner.

Birds, small mammals, amphibians and beneficial insects will come to your landscape and stay if you can provide them with food and shelter. Do a little research into what the critters you want to attract eat or need before deciding what kind of plants to grow.

Native plants work well for attracting the local wildlife. Birds and small animals are accustomed to certain plants for food and shelter. Make sure at least some of the plants in your garden are locally native. These plants will get the wildlife to your garden, and once there, it may be tempted to try some of the other fruit that is not native.

Shelter is important for keeping your resident wildlife happy. Patches of dense shrubs, tall grasses and mature trees provide shelter. Plant windbreaks of conifers and long-lived hardwoods. Grow herbaceous plants, such as ornamental grasses, to provide cover for ground critters. Leave a small pile of twiggy brush in an out-of-the-way place. You can even purchase toad houses and birdhouses from nature stores or garden centres.

Consider installing a bat house. Bats can consume half their weight in insects in one night, and one of their favourites is mosquitoes. The house will need to be in a sunny location about 4.5 m (15') off the ground. Bats will need a water source such as a birdbath.

Provide a source of water. A pond with a shallow side or a birdbath will attract birds and other animals. Frogs and toads eat a wide variety of insect pests and will happily take up residence in or near a ground-level water feature.

In areas where squirrels are not a problem, leave peanuts and seeds out. Place them near a tree, where the squirrels can easily get at them. If you have a large spruce tree, they will eat the seeds out of the cones.

Leave cones out with the other food offerings. The little cone scales that are left when they are done make a great mulch for the garden or can be used to prevent slipping on icy walks and driveways.

Attracting Birds

The following plants will attract certain birds to your garden.

- Ash, crab apple, elderberry, holly, maple and spruce provide cedar waxwings with shelter and food. Birch, cotoneaster, pine and roses are another source of food for them.

- Ash, birch, dogwood, holly and spruce provide food and shelter for chickadees. Oak, pine, rose and sumac are another source of food for them.

- Nectar-producing plants provide food for hummingbirds.

Dogwoods are great plants for attracting all birds. Many bird species enjoy the berries and hunt insects in the branches and on the bark.

Birds will appreciate a place to perch, build nests and escape from felines. Spruce trees, dense shrubs and large hedges will provide that space.

Tall trees will attract migrating birds. The birds land in the tall trees and will fly lower if the inducements are there.

Don't be too hasty to remove dead or dying trees in shelterbelts and wilder areas of your landscape. Birds are attracted to the insects that use dead trees and stumps for breeding and feeding.

Garden and landscape areas that have organic mulch such as bark chips, compost or leaves are great places for birds to forage for insects.

Birds are more likely to visit your yard if you have a source of clean water for them to drink, bathe and frolic in. Provide a place for the birds to perch, such as a few stones in the water that poke above the surface. You can provide a handy water source for birds in areas that freeze in winter by installing a pond or bird-bath heater. The sound of running water in the garden is soothing for us humans. Birds also find the sound appealing, and running water may attract more birds than static water in a birdbath.

Put up lots of bird feeders. A variety of bird feeders and seed will encourage different species of birds to visit your garden. Some birds will visit an elevated feeder, but others prefer a feeder set at or near ground level. Tubular feeders are best because they waste the least amount of feed, protect the feed from the weather and allow only a desired species to feed. Select bird feeders that provide easy access to the feed for birds but exclude scrounging by squirrels. Make sure the feeders are easy to clean and fill, and then keep them clean and full. Feeding the birds in winter encourages them to keep visiting in summer, when they will help keep your insect pest populations under control.

The area around bird feeders can get quite messy with dropped bird seed. Seeds that we fill our bird feeders with are plant seeds that, given the right conditions, will germinate and grow. **Set your bird feeders away from any place you do not want millet, sunflowers and other bird food seeds to grow.**

Attracting Beneficial Bugs

Less than 1% of insect species in Canada are considered to be harmful; many more are actually beneficial. **Insects play many important roles in the landscape, including preying on those few pest species, decomposing organic matter and pollinating your plants.** The ugliest creatures might be the most beneficial ones.

Provide habitat for beneficial insects by planting herbs and other herbaceous, nectar- and pollen-producing plants. Nectar-producing plants that will attract beneficial and predatory insects to your garden include yarrow, coriander, fennel, Queen Anne's lace, lemon gem marigold, sweet alyssum and tansy. Pollen-producing plants such as goldenrod, comfrey, beebalm, salvia, Joe-Pye weed, black-eyed Susan, catmint, purple coneflower, coreopsis and hollyhock will attract beneficial and predatory insects as well.

Savvy gardeners will allow early-season weeds to produce flowers that help attract and feed beneficial and predatory insects and early-season butterflies. Remove or deadhead the weeds before they produce seeds.

Repelling Wildlife

Squirrels and chipmunks are fun to watch, but they can be a rather big problem. They are very ingenious and usually get what they want. Inevitably, squirrels and chipmunks will try to get at your bird feeders. They will eat as much bird seed as they can, leaving little for your feathered friends. They are known to eat hatchlings and bird eggs too, depleting the population of the songbirds you love to listen to. And they will dig up and consume bulbs and other garden plants, which for many gardeners marks the end of their love for these cute little rodents. **One of the easiest ways to control this kind of pest is to have a neat and tidy landscape.** Chipmunks and squirrels love rock piles, stacks of firewood and long grasses. Avoid creating good habitat by minimizing hiding spots.

There are several things you can do to keep your bird seed for the birds. First, purchase bird feeders that are not squirrel friendly. If that isn't enough to deter them, put the feeder where the squirrels cannot reach it, which means 3–3.6 m (10–12') away from any structure that the squirrel might use for a launching point.

Greasing the pole holding the bird feeder works temporarily, but the grease wears off. If squirrels persist in their quest for your bird feeders, mix some cayenne pepper in with the bird seed. The pepper will not bother the birds, but it does deter the squirrels.

Use hardware cloth underneath beds that contain your favourite spring bulbs to deter squirrels. Usually about 20 cm (8") beneath the soil is enough to make an effective barrier. If you are having troubles underneath porches or buildings, simply staple hardware cloth around the edges.

Moles are both friend and foe to your landscape and garden. They eat destructive grubs and leatherjackets, but their tunnelling and the mounds they leave can disrupt plantings and aesthetics. **The only real solution to a mole problem is to trap them out of the area.** Purchase mole traps at your local garden centre or hardware store. Before you can set the traps, you need to determine which tunnels they are frequently using. Destroy part of a tunnel and wait to see if a mole fixes the mess. If one does, then you know you have found an active tunnel, and you can set a trap.

If rabbits, mice and voles are a problem in your garden, you can protect your trees and shrubs over winter with chicken wire. Wrap it around the plant base and higher up the tree or shrub than you expect the snow to reach.

Deer can destroy a wide range of plants, but there are ways to repel them. Hang bars of strongly scented soap or mesh bags of human hair at intervals of 90 cm (36") around the outer branches of trees and shrubs. The hair will need to be replaced every couple of months. Bar soap or hair can be strewn about the ground near herbaceous and other low-growing plants. Other deer repellants include deer predator urine, a spray made of fresh eggs and water and hot pepper sprays.

Sometimes in winter when food is scarce, deer will eat almost anything, and unfortunately, once they have found that your garden is a source of food, it is hard to deter them. **If nothing else works, a fence will keep deer out.** An electric fence will work, as will a regular deer fence.

Domestic cats are not considered to be wildlife, but if you find them to be a problem in your garden, there are simple solutions. **Add coffee grounds to the soil, or stick a number of short twigs in the ground amongst your plants.** The coffee grounds benefit your garden, and the sticks are barely noticeable to you, but both will deter cats from digging in your beds.

Controlling Garden Pests

In a perfectly balanced world, every pest would have a predator. During the normal cycle of life, the pests would flourish until the natural predators caught up and controlled the pests. However, we do not live in a perfect world, and we are not always in balance with nature. Humans interfere with the natural balance by building houses, importing plants and doing other things that change parts of the natural ecosystem. **On the scale of a backyard garden, poor cultural practices can cause pest insects to increase while beneficial critters decrease.** Diseases can also take hold in a poorly managed garden.

Integrated pest management (IPM) is a comprehensive approach to dealing with pests and diseases in your garden. It promotes creating a healthy landscape, monitoring your garden and landscape on a regular basis, learning as much as you can about any insect you find before applying any control measures and using cultural, physical and biological controls before resorting to any chemical use, whether organic or synthetic.

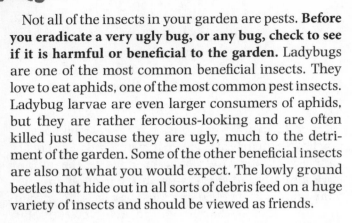

Not all of the insects in your garden are pests. **Before you eradicate a very ugly bug, or any bug, check to see if it is harmful or beneficial to the garden.** Ladybugs are one of the most common beneficial insects. They love to eat aphids, one of the most common pest insects. Ladybug larvae are even larger consumers of aphids, but they are rather ferocious-looking and are often killed just because they are ugly, much to the detriment of the garden. Some of the other beneficial insects are also not what you would expect. The lowly ground beetles that hide out in all sorts of debris feed on a huge variety of insects and should be viewed as friends.

The best way to control any insect or disease problem anywhere is to catch it early. Observe and diagnose problems before they get a firm foothold in your landscape. Take preventative measures to reduce the chance of having problems.

✍ Cultural Controls

Keeping plants healthy and happy is the best way to prevent pests and diseases from causing harm. Grow plants in the conditions they like (soil, light, exposure) and give them what they need (water, fertilizer), even if what they need is to be left alone.

Having a running or flowing water feature as opposed to a stagnant water feature precludes mosquitoes laying their eggs there.

Crop rotation is an effective way of reducing pest problems. The pest's host is no longer where the pest expects it to be, which is especially important for soil-borne diseases.

Always use clean seed, and select varieties that are resistant to typical insect and disease problems.

Till the soil in late fall to expose any pests living or resting near the soil surface. Many pests that survive winter beneath the soil surface will not survive if they are exposed to the rigours of winter.

℔ Physical Controls

Protect your plants with a barrier. Use a floating row cover over your cabbage and kale, netting to keep birds away from tree and shrub fruits, copper strips to stop the forward progress of snails and slugs and toilet paper tubes around seedlings to stop cutworms.

Pick harmful insects off plants or squish them with your fingers as soon as you spot them rather than running for the pesticide.

Bug zappers destroy more beneficial insects than harmful ones. It is best to use traps that are designed specifically for the insects you want to control.

Use beer to bait slugs. Set a shallow dish, bowl or can so the lip of the container is at or just barely above the soil surface and fill it half full with beer. Slugs love beer as much as any Canadian, and they fall in and drown.

Use diatomaceous earth to control soft-bodied pests. It is composed of the skeletons of ancient creatures called diatoms. The skeletons are hard with abrasive, sharp edges that cut and scrape soft insect bodies as the insects move through, which causes the insects to become dehydrated and die.

Protect fruit crops from birds and insects by enclosing the newly set fruit in paper or cheesecloth bags. Avoid plastic because it does not

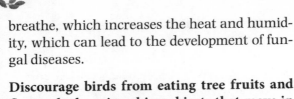

breathe, which increases the heat and humidity, which can lead to the development of fungal diseases.

Discourage birds from eating tree fruits and flowers by hanging shiny objects that move in the wind, such as aluminum pie plates or strips of foil. Be aware that this won't work forever; birds will soon figure out that the objects pose no danger to them.

𝒟 Biological Controls

Many types of biological controls are quite effective. The biological control might be a predator, a parasite or a pathogen.

Like all living things, pests are susceptible to disease-causing organisms such as bacteria, viruses and fungi. However, most insect pathogens are relatively specific to certain groups of insects and certain life stages. They are not instantaneously effective, and their effectiveness is dependent on both the host abundance and environmental conditions. Note that this type of control can be used at the same time as parasitic and predatory controls. One form of a pathogenic biological control is the naturally occurring soil bacterium *Bacillus thuringiensis* var. *kurstaki*, or Btk for short. It breaks down the gut lining of some insect pests. However, Btk can harm or kill many beneficial insects, and large applications are not a good idea. Small spot applications of very small amounts may be acceptable. Btk is available in garden centres.

Predators usually have a favourite prey, and although some will consume only that prey, others will consume a number of other pests as well.

A predator might consume large numbers of prey during one or all stages of its life cycle. So depending on the number of pests, some species of predators will provide good control while others may provide good control only at certain times of the year. Sometimes they will only suppress or keep a pest infestation under control. Some common predators include ladybugs, lacewings, mites and flies.

Parasites, or parasitoids to be technically correct, have an immature life stage that develops within a single insect host, which ultimately kills the host. They attack a certain stage of the pest's life cycle, breaking up the life cycle and thus reducing the overall numbers of the pest. They are specialized in their choice of host and are generally much smaller than their host. Parasitoids are usually wasps or flies but are occasionally another type of insect.

Biological control agents are becoming widely available. **You can purchase ladybugs, lacewings, *Trichogramma* wasps, nematodes and a host of other beneficial insects and microorganisms to control pest populations.**

Chemical Controls

Make sure to properly identify insects before reaching for the insecticide. Ladybugs, lacewings and a plethora of other beneficial insects may be killed, and you will lose their free pest control services.

A mild soap and water spray is very effective at reducing infestations of aphids and mites. You might have to repeat your application a week or so later (depending on the pest), and make sure to rinse the plants with fresh water an hour or so after spraying the soap solution.

Dormant (also called horticultural) oils are sprayed on dormant fruit and shade trees, shrubs and vines in winter to control insects such as scale insects and aphids. The oils suffocate the insects and their eggs and are of low toxicity to humans. Follow the directions carefully to avoid harming beneficial insects.

Organic pesticides break down rapidly and will not persist in the environment. Many organic pesticides (botanicals) are made from compounds derived from plants and can be more toxic than synthetic pesticides. **Any pesticide should be used as a last resort.**

A Few Last Tips

Environmental Gardening

Organic Gardening

The news is full of what pesticides and synthetic fertilizers do to your health. With the growing trend to produce our own food without pesticides comes increased interest in organic gardening. So what is organic gardening? **Most people agree that organic gardening is the process of growing fruits, vegetables and ornamentals naturally, without man-made inputs.** However, people's opinions differ as to what constitutes a man-made input. For example, is organic fertilizer acceptable? It's technically man-made, but with organic ingredients.

How you personally choose to garden organically might be different than how your friends or fellow gardeners do. But no matter the method, one of the first steps is to ensure your soil is healthy and able to support the growth of the plants you choose to grow. Soil building and conservation are a necessary part of organic gardening. **One easy way to improve your soil is to add organic matter.** Any kind of organic matter is good, but compost is a great choice. Compost adds not only the organic matter, but also a host of nutrients. For long-term soil health and to manage your soil, you need to keep the nutrient levels at a satisfactory level.

If you need additional fertilization, use organic fertilizer that contains the macronutrients needed for plant growth. Those macronutrients (nitrogen, phosphorus and potassium) are needed by the plants in

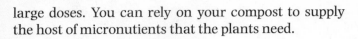

large doses. You can rely on your compost to supply the host of micronutrients that the plants need.

To keep pest problems under control, try to practice good cropping techniques. Rotate your crops to ensure that similar crops are not grown in the same place year after year. Crop rotation helps control pest problems naturally because pests cannot find their hosts. Observe your garden continuously to be sure to catch any kind of infestation quickly. Most often, if you catch a problem when it is still relatively small, the treatment is less intensive and more successful.

Natural Landscaping

It is fashionable these days to be closer to nature. The practice of natural landscaping has taken hold and is not likely to disappear. No type of landscaping is really natural because it is a modification of the outdoors to serve the people. This is done by planting, by altering the contours of the ground and by building structures. Natural landscaping does not mean converting your landscape back to what is was originally. **Natural landscaping does mean using a wide array of landscaping techniques that help retain natural landscape features, including wetlands, woodlands and natural drainage features.**

Natural landscaping has many benefits. A mostly natural landscape will require few pesticides, little fertilizer and less water to maintain. It may even cost less to install than a non-natural landscape. Once it is established, it will combat erosion and will accommodate storm and flood waters better than a landscape full of non-native plants that may not be built to withstand local conditions.

Using native plants is never a bad decision. Native plants have evolved over thousands of years in a particular region. They have adapted to the geography, hydrology and climate that is specific to that region. Using native plants, including wildflowers and grasses, wher-ever you can is in the long run a more economical alter-native to conventional landscaping because they are readily available and are low maintenance. As a bonus, native plants will provide habitat for a variety of native wildlife species such as songbirds and butterflies.

If you live in an urban area, you may not be able to create a totally natural landscape, but you can include aspects of a natural landscape in your more traditional urban landscape. For example, blend your traditional backyard lawn into a naturalized meadow with native wildflowers, trees, shrubs and native grasses.

Sustainable Landscaping

A sustainable landscape conserves resources and reduces labour inputs. It should be economical to both implement and maintain. Chemical applications will be reduced, as will the water needed to maintain the landscape.

There are five basic considerations if you choose to design your landscape as a sustainable one. It has to be functional, able to be maintained with relative ease and environmentally sound. The cost and the visual appeal of a sustainable landscape are less important than the other three considerations, but important nonetheless.

☞ Plant to Save Energy

With the rising costs (both economically and environmentally) of fossil fuels, it is important to create a landscape that saves energy. **Trees can help conserve energy if they are planted in the correct location.** Properly placed trees can reduce your energy costs by 25%, with some landscapes showing an energy savings of up to 50%. Plant trees so they provide plenty of shade in summer but also shelter from cold winds in winter.

During those hot summer days, a lot of the heat that enters our homes will come through the windows. The sun is high in the sky during summer, so windows on the east and west will let in almost as much solar energy as windows on the south side. **Use trees to help shade the east and west windows.** The trees will have to be within about 8 m (25') of the house and reach at least 3 m (10') higher than the windows to provide adequate shade. Avoid shading the south-facing windows to allow the maximum solar energy to enter the house in winter.

Other areas that you might consider shading include air conditioners, any hard surface areas, your parking spot and any areas you will frequent during the heat of the day. The canopy formed by the trees will cool the surface area in your landscape.

The ideal shade tree is large, with a dense, reaching canopy and fine twigs. Grow the biggest tree that space will allow, but ensure that its needs meet the growing conditions of the site to ensure a long life. Do not choose any tree that has a short lifespan or is susceptible to pests or diseases.

During winter, the heating bill can become rather high when the temperatures drop rather low. **Save on your heating bill by keeping your south-facing windows unshaded.** A significant amount of solar energy can be gained even in the middle of winter from the sun shining through south-facing windows. Depending on the orientation of the house, you can even realize some solar gain on the east and west sides. If you use this solar energy, you can make up to 20% of the energy needed to heat your home.

The force of the winter wind can also increase the cost of heating your home. If the cold air can get in, the warm air can get out. **A windbreak of trees will block those extremely cold winter winds and keep your house warmer, which will reduce your energy consumption.** Some evergreens should be included in the windbreak for the best winter protection. The semi-solid barrier provided by evergreens will give better protection than a completely solid barrier.

Most places will have different directions for prevailing winds in the summer season and the winter season. **The prevailing wind in winter in Canada is from the northwest, so plant your windbreak on that side of the house.** Plant the windbreak to run perpendicular to the prevailing wind. To help you decide how far from the house to plant, keep in mind that downwind from the windbreak, the area up to a distance of 10 times the height of the windbreak will be an area of relative calm and an area up to a distance of 25 times the height of the windbreak will have some reduction in wind.

If space is limited, then you will likely not have enough room to have the ultimate windbreak. **Even a canopy of large deciduous trees will provide shelter.** For the best effect, the canopy in your yard should cover about half the available space.

Other plantings around the house can also help reduce energy costs. **Plant outside the eaves to allow rainfall to naturally water your plants, but also to create a dead air space that will actually help insulate the home.** Vines on a trellis attached to the house will work in a similar

fashion. In summer, less heat from the sun will be conducted into the home, and in winter, less wind will hit the house directly.

Plant to Save Water

Lawn areas are the highest consumers of water. **Reduce the amount of turf in the landscape to reduce the amount of water that will be necessary.** Plan for turf to be placed only in areas that are going to be used as turf—for example, a play area for children. Choose low-maintenance, water-efficient groundcovers to replace high-maintenance turf in areas that will not have foot traffic. For areas that are in turf, mow the lawn a bit higher to slightly reduce the amount of water that the lawn will need.

Choosing the appropriate plants is important in a sustainable landscape. **Native plants are always a good choice, but they are not the only choice.** Spring-flowering bulbs are seasonal drought evaders and deserve a place in your landscape. They will complete their lifecycle in spring when there is generally more moisture available. During the hot, dry summer, they are dormant, so they avoid the less favourable time of year.

Xeric plants are a good choice in a sustainable landscape. A xeric plant is any plant that can withstand drought better than most other plants. Sometimes plants have root systems that are better able to access moisture. Bur oak trees have a tap root and can access water from deeper aquifers than trees with spreading, relatively shallow root systems. Xeric plants may have smaller, more rounded and needle-like leaves and may also have a thick, waxy cuticle or many small hairs on their leaves so that they lose less water through transpiration than the average plant. Mugo pines have narrow, needle-like leaves that reduce transpiration. Sedum leaves have a waxy coating that helps them reduce transpiration. Coral bells will actually hang on to tiny droplets of water with the many hairs on the underside of their leaves. Other plants will even store water as a mechanism against drought.

Indoor Gardening

Plants transform a house into a home. They make your indoor space more comfortable and most definitely more attractive. They soften the architectural lines inside the house in the same fashion as outdoor plants do in the landscape surrounding the house.

Houseplants are more than just attractive—they clean the air in our homes. Many dangerous and common toxins, such as benzene, formaldehyde and trichloroethylene are absorbed and eliminated by houseplants. **A few of the easiest, toxin-absorbing houseplants to grow are spider plant, peace lily, pot mums, English ivy, weeping fig, Chinese evergreen, dragon tree, snake plant and gerbera daisy.**

Look for creative ways to display your plants and add beauty to your home. Indoor fountains and moisture-loving plants such as a peace lily in a vase of water are interesting and attractive look at. They add a decorative touch to a houseplant display.

General Maintenance

Group plants with the same needs together in large containers to more easily meet the needs of the plants. Cacti can be planted together in a gritty soil mix and

placed in a dry, bright location. Moisture- and humidity-loving plants can be planted in a large terrarium, where moisture levels remain higher.

Just as you did for the garden outdoors, match your indoor plants to the conditions your home provides. If a room receives little light, consider houseplants that require very low light levels, and vice versa. Low-light-tolerant plants include philodendron, cast iron plant and snake plant. Bright-light-tolerant plants include cactus, jade plant and goldfish plant.

When growing plants indoors, there are three aspects of interior light to consider: intensity, duration and quality. Intensity is the difference between a south-facing window with full sun and a north-facing room with no direct sunlight. Duration is how long the light lasts in a specific location. An east-facing window will have a shorter duration of light than a south-facing window. Quality refers to the spectrum of the light. Natural light provides a broader spectrum than artificial light.

Many common houseplants dislike hot, dry conditions and will thrive in cooler, more moist conditions than you will provide in your home. **Avoid placing houseplants in hot or cold drafts, always turn thermostats down at night and provide moist conditions by sitting pots on pebble trays.** Water in the pebble tray will evaporate but won't soak excessively into the soil of the pot because the pebbles hold the pot above the water. Plants that like humid conditions may do best in your bathroom, where showering and the toilet bowl full of water maintain higher moisture levels than in any other room.

Watering is a key element to houseplant care. Over-watering can be as much of a problem as under-watering. As you do with your garden plants, water thoroughly and infrequently. Let the soil dry out a bit before watering plants. Some plants are the exception to this rule. **Find out what the water requirements of** your houseplants are so you will have an idea of how frequently or infrequently you will need to water.

Houseplants generally need fertilizer only when they are actively growing. Always use a weak fertilizer to avoid burning the roots. Never feed plants when they are very dry. Moisten the soil and then feed them a couple of days later.

When repotting, go up by only one size at a time. In general, the new pot should be no more than 5–10 cm (2–4") larger in diameter than the previous pot. If you find your soil drying out too frequently, then you may wish to use a larger pot that will stay moist longer.

Check houseplants regularly for common indoor pests such as whiteflies, spider mites and mealybugs. Our dry indoor air is the perfect environment for the growth of many critters that we would rather not host. Most indoor plant pests can be controlled by wiping leaves with a damp sponge. More difficult pests can be controlled with insecticidal soap.

Seasonal Care

Pay attention to the needs of the plants in relation to the amount of light they receive. Reduce watering of houseplants in winter because most of them need little water when the days are so short and the growth rate is slow.

During the winter months in more severe climates, the humidity level in our homes is very low. **Most indoor plants will benefit from increased humidity levels.** Place pots on a tray of pebbles and fill the tray with water. If you add water when needed, you will increase the humidity through evaporation but prevent waterlogged roots.

Dust on plants is more than just an eyesore. It prevents plants from making full use the light they receive.

Clean the foliage of your houseplants regularly, but particularly in the winter months. When light levels are low, it is important for plants to be able to use whatever light is available. As a bonus, you might reduce insect populations because their eggs will likely be wiped off along with the dust. Rinsing the dust off with water is also a good method of removal, but make sure not to do this to plants with hairy leaves.

As the days of spring start to lengthen, indoor plants may start to show signs of new growth. **Increase watering and apply weak (quarter-strength) fertilizer only after they begin to grow.**

Many houseplants enjoy spending summer outside. The brighter the location you need to provide for your plant indoors, the more likely it is to do well outdoors. Avoid putting plants in direct sun outside because they will have a hard time adjusting to the intensity of light and then the lack of light when they are moved back inside at the end of summer. Begin to harden off any houseplants you plan to move outdoors a couple of weeks prior to actually putting them out for good.

Check houseplants that spent summer outdoors for insect pests before moving them back indoors for winter. Even the most carefully checked plant will often carry some critters.

Herb Care

Winter can be long for gardeners who love to keep their fingers in the soil, and in the dead of winter, green growth of any kind is welcome. **Growing herbs indoors over winter will not only satisfy your green thumb, it will also provide wonderful scents and fresh, home-grown herbs to use in your cooking year-round.** Choose herbs that you will use and that are compact in size so they don't get too large for your growing area.

Most herbs are sun worshipers. **Any herbs you are growing indoors, particularly throughout winter, should be kept in the brightest window you have to prevent them from becoming too straggly or dying.**

Even if you place your herbs in direct sunlight, you may have to provide supplemental light to keep them healthy. To ensure that the whole spectrum of light is available for growth, use three cool white fluorescent bulbs with one warm white bulb. Place the lights directly above the herbs, about 20 cm (8") from the lowest leaves. If possible, install the lights on small chains so you can easily adjust the distance between the light and the plants.

Although light is the most important factor for success, don't neglect your herbs' other needs. Herbs almost always like good drainage, so ensure your soil mixture will drain quite quickly. Feed your herbs once a week while they are actively growing, and water thoroughly but infrequently. Wait until the soil is dry to the touch before you water so that you do not drown your herbs before you have a chance to enjoy them.

The following herbs are consistently compact and have great flavour:

- 'Fernleaf' dill (*Anethum graveolens*) germinates in 7 to 14 days at room temperature and grows up to 45 cm (18") tall

- 'Spicy Globe' basil (*Ocimum basilicum minimum*) is a dense herb that germinates in 6 to 12 days at room temperature and grows about 20 cm (8") tall

- Greek oregano (*Origanum vulgare hirtum*) germinates in 7 to 21 days at room temperature and grows 20–30 cm (8–12") tall

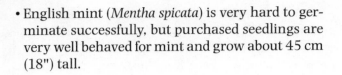

• English mint (*Mentha spicata*) is very hard to germinate successfully, but purchased seedlings are very well behaved for mint and grow about 45 cm (18") tall.

Enjoying the Fruits of Your Labour

Decorating

The best time to cut flowers for arrangements and bouquets is early in the morning while the temperature is still cool. Cut the flower stems at an angle, then immediately place the cut flowers into a vase with warm water.

To force spring bloomers, cut branches of dormant flowering shrubs, such as forsythia, crab apple and cherry, to bring indoors. Placed in a bright location in a vase of water, they will begin to flower, giving you a taste of spring in winter.

If you have healthy willows, dogwoods, Virginia creeper or evergreens, cut a few branches to use in Christmas wreaths.

If you had a real Christmas tree, instead of recycling it, cut it up and use the branches as a mulch to shelter low-growing shrubs and groundcovers.

Eating

Fruits, vegetables and other plant parts that you intend to eat should not be sprayed with pesticides of any kind.

There is a window of time to harvest your produce. You need to give it time to mature, but you don't want to wait too long and risk frost damage or let it get past its prime. **Know when to harvest your produce.** Harvest any soft fruits or vegetables before the first frost in fall to prevent frost damage. Cool weather vegetables such as carrots, cabbage, Brussels sprouts and turnips can wait awhile longer because they are frost hardy.

Use care when handling your harvested vegetables and fruits. Any damage such as bruising or cuts can shorten the shelf life of your harvest.

Proper storage can lengthen the shelf life of your harvest. **Store your fruits and vegetables at cool temperatures and high humidity to ensure the longest possible shelf life.** When a fruit or vegetable is picked or harvested, the respiration process is still occurring. During this process, sugars and other compounds are broken down, releasing heat, water and carbon dioxide and eventually causing your produce to wilt and spoil. Usually, the higher the temperature, the greater the respiration rate and the less time the produce can be stored. The respiration rate also varies with the amount of water that is contained in the product. Produce with a high water content, such as lettuce, will respire much more rapidly than produce with a low water content, such as potatoes, so it will have a shorter shelf life, even when stored in a cool place.

Consider donating extra produce to a homeless shelter or food bank, where it will be much appreciated.

℧ Harvesting Guide

- **Asparagus:** spears are ready when they are more than 15 cm (6") above the ground but before the heads open. Snap off the spears at the soil line. Expect to enjoy fresh asparagus for about six weeks in spring. It will keep for about a week in the fridge.

- **Beans:** pick before they are totally developed, usually beginning about three weeks after the first bloom. If you leave the beans on the plant to size up for seed, then the plant will stop producing beans. They will keep for up to a week in the fridge.

- **Beets:** harvest them before they are 5 cm (2") in diameter. The roots will keep for about two weeks and the greens for about one week in the fridge.

- **Broccoli:** cut it about 15 cm (6") below the flower head when it is fully developed but before the flowers open. Broccoli heads will keep for about a week in the fridge.

- **Brussels sprouts:** harvest individual sprouts from the base of the plant upward when they are 2.5–4 cm (1–1.5") in diameter and still tender and green. For the longest shelf life, keep them close to freezing and at high humidity. Brussels sprouts will keep for about three weeks in the fridge.

- **Cabbage:** harvest when the heads are solid but intact; they tend to split once they get too large. Cut just beneath the head. Cabbage will keep for a few weeks in the fridge.

- **Carrots:** for best flavour, dig them up before they are 2.5 cm (1") in diameter, but for the longest storage life, leave them in the ground until the first frost. Carrots will keep for a few weeks in the fridge. For longer storage, pack them in damp sand and store them at just above freezing with high humidity.

- **Corn:** harvest sweet corn when the kernels are in the milk stage. The kernels should be bright yellow. The silks will be dry and brown when the cob is ready for eating. Sweet corn does not store without some sort of processing.

- **Cucumbers:** if you are making dill pickes, pick the cucumbers when they are quite small. For fresh eating, you will want them small but easy to peel; don't let them get over-mature. Cucumbers will keep for a few days in the fridge.

- **Lettuce:** pick both leaf lettuce and head lettuce when small. The leaves should be tender and sweet. Lettuce will keep for a few days in the fridge.

- **Muskmelon:** harvest when a crack appears around the base of the fruit stem. At this time, the fruit will readily separate. Muskmelon will keep for a couple of weeks in the fridge.

- **Onions:** cut fresh green onion while it is small. If you want onions for storage, dig up the bulbs when they are about 5 cm (2") in diameter. The mature stalks will weaken and might even fall over when the onions are ready. Let the onions cure for a few days, then store them at room temperature or slightly cooler with good air circulation.

- **Parsnips:** harvest after a hard frost or in early spring prior to any new growth starting. If you are leaving your parsnips in the ground over winter, place a few centimetres of soil mulch over them in late fall to ensure the parsnips are not exposed. If you dig them up in fall, store them at just above freezing at high humidity, and they should keep for four to six months. Parsnips will keep for a few weeks in the fridge.

- **Peas:** pick when fully developed but not overripe. Once the pod is totally mature, the peas will have lost their best flavour. Pick peas with edible pods while the seeds are less than fully developed— usually while the pod is still flat. Peas will keep for a couple of weeks in the fridge.

- **Peppers:** harvest when they are still firm. If left on the plant they will eventually all turn red. Peppers will keep for a few days in the fridge.

- **Potatoes:** for fresh eating, once they're big enough, dig them up as you want them. For storage, harvest when they are full sized and have firm skins. For best storage they need to be well dried and then kept at a few degrees above freezing at about 70% humidity.

- **Pumpkins:** see squash.

- **Radishes:** dig them up when still small, or they will become quite tough and woody. They will keep for a few days in the fridge.

- **Rhubarb:** harvest throughout the growing season when the stalks are firm.

- **Spinach:** pick while still young for the best flavour. Spinach will continue to produce if you pick the leaves regularly. It will keep for a few days in the fridge.

- **Squash:** harvest summer squash, such as zucchini, when the fruit is young and tender. At peak harvest, your fingernail should easily mark the rind. Harvest winter squash, such as pumpkins, acorn squash and spaghetti squash, when they are mature but before the first frost. The rind should be hard enough that your fingernail will not puncture it easily. If they don't have time to ripen in the garden, they will ripen off the vine. Leave a bit of stem on the squash to help extend the storage life. Cure winter squash in a cool, frost-free location before storing them for winter at 13–16° C (55–60° F) with about 70% humidity. However, if you want to use them right away, squash will ripen fastest at room temperature.

- **Tomatoes:** should not be picked until ripe, but if you live in a climate that has a short summer, you may have to pick your tomatoes while they are still green. Pick them at the green mature stage—the flesh will appear a bit translucent—and they will ripen off the vine. They can be stored at about 13° C (55° F) at 90% humidity for a few days.

• **Zucchini:** see squash.

Fun With Kids

The whole family can share the joy of gardening. **Garden with your kids as a learning experience and for fun.** Children are natural gardeners—they learn by doing...and love to play in the dirt.

Think back to your gardening experiences as a child. **If you remember gardening as a rather unpleasant chore, think about what would have made it fun.** Gardening should be a positive experience, teaching children patience and an appreciation of the natural world. It could be a doorway to healthy living for their entire lives.

There are many activities you can do with the young folk in the garden. **The process of gardening not only brings to the children the satisfaction of caring for something and watching it grow, but it is also a great way to explore how nature works.**

Here are some suggestions for fun things kids can do in the garden:

• grow sunflowers and measure how tall they are in relation to the child

• build a fort with the stems of tall sunflowers tied together at the top, or a teepee constructed of bamboo poles covered in vines such as scarlet runner beans

- grow flowers and plants that tend to be the most interesting in the dark, such as moonflowers

- grow miniature plants, such as baby pumpkins, baby corn or ornamental flowers, that remain tiny even when mature, for a realistic sense of scale for the kids

- grow plants that produce flowers that they can pick for bouquets for their teachers and friends

- plant the carrot patch in the shape of the letter of the child's first name

- create a rainbow garden with rows of flowers in rainbow colours; use white flowers to create clouds around the rainbow.

Let very young children begin their gardening experience by digging in the dirt. Together you can explore the earth for worms and other creatures. Give slightly older children a few fast-growing seeds to plant, and check them each day to see what has sprouted. They will be amazed at how fast some plants can grow. Give older children their own little garden spot and let them plant whatever they want. It does not matter how it looks as long as they can participate in sowing, nurturing and harvesting the plants. **Get your children involved in gardening early in life so they will cherish the experience for the rest of their lives.**

Glossary

Acidic soil: soil with a pH lower than 7.0

Aerobic: living or occurring only in the presence of oxygen

Alkaline soil: soil with a pH higher than 7.0

Anaerobic: living or occurring in an environment without oxygen

Annual: a plant that germinates, flowers, sets seed and dies in one growing season

Basal leaves: leaves that form from the crown

Basal rosette: a ring or rings of leaves growing from the crown of a plant at or near ground level; flowering stems of such plants grow separately from the crown

Berm: a mound of earth, or earth and debris

Bog plant: a plant that thrives in wet soil

Bolting: when a plant produces flowers and seeds prematurely

Bract: a modified leaf at the base of a flower or flower cluster

Corm: a bulb-like, food-storing, underground stem resembling a bulb without scales

Crown: the part of the plant at or just below soil level where the shoots join the roots

Cultivar: a *culti*vated plant *vari*ety with one or more distinct differences from the parent species, e.g., in flower colour, leaf variation or disease resistance

Damping off: fungal disease causing seedlings to rot at soil level and then topple over

Deadhead: to remove spent flowers to maintain a neat appearance and encourage a longer blooming period

Direct sow: to plant seeds straight into the garden, in the location you want the plants to grow

Disbud: to remove some flowerbuds to improve the size or quality of the remaining ones

Dormancy: a period of plant inactivity, usually during winter or other unfavourable climatic conditions

Double flower: a flower with an unusually large number of petals, often caused by mutation of the stamens into petals

Emergent: a plant that grows in deep water, with its stems, leaves and flowers above the water surface and its roots below

Espalier: a tree trained from a young age to grow on a single plane

Genus: category of biological classification between the species and family levels; the first word in a scientific name indicates the genus, e.g., *Digitalis* in *Digitalis purpurea*

Grafting: a type of propagation in which a stem or bud of one plant is joined onto the rootstock of another plant of a closely related species

Hardy: capable of surviving cold weather or frost without protection

Hip: the fruit of a rose, containing the seeds

Humus: decomposed or decomposing organic material in the soil

Hybrid: a plant resulting from natural or human-induced crossbreeding between varieties, species or genera; the hybrid expresses features of each parent plant

Inflorescence: an arrangement of flowers on a single stem

Invasive: able to spread aggressively from the planting site and outcompete other plants

Knot garden: a formal design, often used for herb gardens, in which low, clipped hedges are arranged in elaborate, knot-like patterns

Loam: a loose soil composed of clay, sand and organic matter, often highly fertile

Marginal: a plant that grows in shallow water, with its stems, leaves and flowers above the water surface and its leaves below

Mulch: a material, (e.g. shredded bark, pine cones, leaves, straw), used to surround a plant to protect it from weeds, cold or heat and to promote moisture retention

Neutral soil: soil with a pH of 7.0

Node: the area on a stem from which a leaf or new shoot grows

Offset: a young plantlet that naturally sprouts around the base of the parent plant and produces new plants from buds at its tips

Oxygenator: a submerged plant that releases oxygen into the water and reduces algae growth in the pond

Panicle: a compound flower structure with groups of flowers on short stalks

Perennial: a plant that takes three or more years to complete its life cycle

pH: a measure of acidity or alkalinity (the lower the pH, the higher the acidity); the pH of soil influences availability of nutrients for plants

Plantlet: a young or small plant

Rhizome: a root-like, usually swollen, food-storing stem that grows horizontally at or just below soil level, from which new shoots and true roots may emerge

Rootball: the root mass and surrounding soil of a plant

Rosette: see Basal rosette

Seedhead: dried, inedible fruit that contains seeds; the fruiting stage of the inflorescence

Self-seeding: reproducing by means of seeds without human assistance, so that new plants constantly replace those that die

Semi-double flower: a flower with petals in two or three rings

Semi-hardy: a plant capable of surviving the climatic conditions of a given region if protected

Single flower: a flower with a single ring of typically four or five petals

Spathe: a leaf-like bract that encloses a flower cluster or spike

Species: the original plant from which cultivars are derived; the fundamental unit of biological classification, indicated by a two-part scientific name, e.g., *Digitalis purpurea* (*purpurea* is the specific epithet)

Sport: an atypical plant or part of a plant that arises through mutation; some sports are horticulturally desirable and propagated as new cultivars

Standard: a shrub or small tree grown with an erect main stem, accomplished either through pruning and training or by grafting the plant onto a tall, straight stock

Submerged: a plant that grows underwater

Subshrub: a perennial plant that is somewhat shrubby, with a woody basal stem; its upper parts are herbaceous and die back each year

Subspecies (subsp.): a naturally occurring, regional form of a species, often isolated from other subspecies but still potentially interfertile with them

Sucker: a shoot that comes up from the root, often some distance from the plant; it can be separated to form a new plant once it develops its own roots

Taproot: a root system consisting of one main vertical root with smaller roots branching from it

Tender: incapable of surviving harsher climatic conditions of a given region; requires protection from frost or cold

True: describes the passing of desirable characteristics from the parent plant to seed-grown offspring; also called breeding true to type

Tuber: a swollen part of a rhizome or root bearing nodes and buds, containing food stores for the plant

Umbel: flowers on stalks, radiating in a U shape from a single point at the top of a stem, e.g., dill flowers

Understorey plant: a plant that prefers to grow beneath the canopies of trees in a woodland setting

Variegation: describes foliage that has more than one colour, often patched or striped or bearing differently coloured leaf margins

Variety (var.): a naturally occurring variant of a species; below the level of subspecies in biological classification

About the Authors

Patricia Hanbidge is the principal of the newest horticultural school on the Prairies—the Saskatoon School of Horticulture. She has been in the horticultural industry for over 25 years as a consultant, popular weekly newspaper columnist, teacher and author. For years, Patricia coordinated the Master Gardener Program, the Prairie Horticulture Certificate Program and the GardenLine Information Service at the University of Saskatchewan and was the horticultural editor for the *Gardener for the Prairies* magazine. Her company Green Schemes & Scapes specializes in horticultural consulting and landscape design. She has a strong interest in educating the public to use more sustainable alternatives while gardening. Patricia is also a well-known and talented speaker both locally and internationally. Last but not least, Patricia also hosts garden tours around the world.

Alison Beck has gardened since she was a child. She has a diploma in Horticulture from Niagara College and a degree in Creative Writing from York University. Alison has written or co-written 36 best-selling gardening guides. Her books showcase her talent for practical advice and her passion for gardening.

Laura Peters is a certified Master Gardener with 26 gardening books to her credit. She has valuable experience in every aspect of the horticultural industry in a career that has spanned more than 17 years. Also a native Albertan, she enjoys sharing her practical knowledge of organic gardening, plant varieties and gardening products with fellow prairie gardeners.

Veteran garden writer Don Williamson is the author or coauthor of 24 popular gardening guides. He has a degree in horticultural technology from Olds College and lots of practical experience in the design and construction of perennial and annual beds in formal landscape settings.